HOCKEY,
eh?

TRUE CONFESSIONS OF A MIDLIFE RINK RAT

MEAGAN HESHAM

STRENGTH
PRESS

www.strengthpressbooks.com

Paperback: ISBN 978-1-7781962-0-1

Audiobook: ISBN 978-1-7781962-2-5

Ebook: ISBN 978-1-7781962-1-8

First paperback edition June 2022

Edited by Pat Beaven & Susan Gaigher

Cover by Xee Designs

Photographs by Pat Beaven, Zak Hesham, Will Hesham, Meagan Hesham
Strength Press

Toronto, Canada

www.strengthpressbooks.com

Contents

One

Pre-Enlightenment

S weat trickles down from my helmet and stings my eyes as I take a long, frosty inhale. I smack my stick down on the ice like I mean business. Bending my knees into a squat, I put on my best hockey scowl as I face off against this six-foot giant. My opponent seems serious in stance, but beyond the cold metal cage of his helmet, I detect laughter in his mischievous eyes. Laughing at *me*? The puck drops quicker than I'm ready for, and I've already lost it. My burly opponent stick-handles the puck down the ice—all fancy footwork, edging, and crossovers. I try to poke-check. I even try to nudge him into the boards a little to interrupt his show, but he continues faking me out, deking from left to right. Whoosh! He passes the puck through my skates. He shoots, he scores! Sliding along on one knee, he does a celebratory fist pump, "Oh yeah!" He cuts that short, spins around, and throws his arm around my shoulder as we glide off the ice. "Don't worry. You'll get it next time, Mom!"

My girly ten-year-old self would never in a million years have believed that I would be there, in that arena, geared-up-massive shoulder pads and all - playing hockey with the boys! And the idea that hockey would turn out to play such a big role in my adult life was inconceivable. Growing up, I had no clue about hockey. The Toronto area I grew up in wasn't a *hockey neighbourhood*. Or maybe it was, but I just didn't know it. I don't think I even knew anyone who played hockey. Back in middle school, the only *athletes* my friends and I were interested in watching were our cutey-crushes. We'd sit alongside the school field or on the stairs by the outdoor basketball hoop to watch the action at lunch and after school. There were no community arenas nearby that I knew of. Although sometimes there would be an uneven, kind of bumpy outdoor rink made behind the school where we skated at lunchtime and after the 3:30 dismissal bell. Girls glided around as elegantly as possible in their white figure skates, while boys showed off with their snow-jobs, spraying ice all over us with their side stops. I even had a skating birthday party one year. But no one would have called me *sporty*.

I could always be found in skirts and dresses, never pants, which I absolutely refused to wear until I was about eleven. My big passion was dancing. Sports, especially team sports, and gym class, were activities to be avoided at all costs. I hated gym so much that in grade seven, I joined band and learned to play the clarinet just because it conflicted with gym on my schedule and meant I could skip gym for band class!

My parents are both originally from Montreal, and I recall hearing that my dad used to play and coach hockey at some point but had to give it up because of his super-arched feet, which I inherited. That was the extent of my hockey knowledge or *involvement* despite having grown up in what might have been considered a typical Canadian family. If there really is such a thing.

My husband, born in Egypt with a Syrian background, has always been impressed by what he sees as my full-on Canadian-ness. He jokes that it was the reason he fell for me, just like he had fallen in love with hockey in the eighth grade. Come to Canada, throw on a Leafs sweatshirt, and hook up with a super-Canadian chick. Ah, the dream! To my husband, I seem like a pure-bred Canadian going back a lot of generations. I guess that really is accurate. When people ask me about my background, it often goes like this:

"Where are you from?"

"Canada."

"But your parents, where are they from?"

"Canada."

Then I assume they're looking for a more interesting answer, because they follow with ...

"Your grandparents?"

"Canada."

"Well, then, what's *their* background? Why do you look so European? You *must* be something other than just Canadian!"

Conversations like this made me feel boring. Going way back, my background is a mix of various things like Scottish and Irish. I'm not sure if people were looking for a twist—or a surprise—to find out I'm half something-or-other. Or maybe I'm projecting because I guess I always felt it was pretty boring to be *just* Canadian.

Sure, maple leaves are stunning when autumn turns the scenery all golden, red, and glowy. But soon winter follows, and I never loved winter. Or skiing. Or cottaging. The only truly Canadian thing I've been able to embrace is maple syrup, which I'm all in for—100%! I just never identified strongly with being Canadian.

All my life I've been drawn to the more exotic, like belly dance, curry, Bollywood movies, reggaeton, Muay Thai, my husband—basically things that were the opposites of my *boring* Canadian culture. Because Canada is such a multicultural country, it's easy to experience different and exciting cultural arts, traditions, and cuisines. Much like a child who ends up being the polar opposite of everything their parents are, I was running away as fast and hard as I could from my whole Canadian-ness, remaking myself into what I thought were other, much more beautiful, characters. I dyed my dirty blond hair a shiny black, wore tons of kohl eye paint, and signed up for Hindi language classes at the local high school. I studied, performed, and later taught Raks Sharqi, known in the West as belly dance. As a teenager, I spent time in Latin dance clubs, perfecting my salsa moves to music that I loved. And I didn't meet the man who would become my husband at Timmies or a hockey game. As teens, we met through Egyptian dance and music. I was a dancer, and he was a drummer for Arabesque, a Toronto-based Egyptian performance company. We bonded over our mad love of Arabic music; he was the first guy I had gone out with that I could have deep conversations with about Arabic music, culture, and the latest Egyptian hot spots in town. Our first date was shawarmas and mango juice. Our second date was at an out-of-town Arabic music store he knew I would love. He had just come to Canada from Egypt with his family a year before I met him, so he was still Arabic enough for me; not all Canadianized yet, other than the Maple Leafs sweatshirt he proudly wore the day I first spoke to him. This was so fresh for me. I was used to Canadian boys with their skateboarding and Converse runners, and along came this Arabic boy who understood everything I loved at the time and had a whole other energy to him, which was super attractive to me. He gifted me with a personalized gold necklace on our first date for goodness' sake—not a usual Canadian dating move!

After dating for five years, I finally married this lover of all things Canadian! Another four years passed quickly as we grew into life together. In all that time I don't remember us ever talking about hockey or even referencing our *national sport*. That is until our first baby boy came along. Looking back, there were clues I might have missed; the Toronto Maple Leafs sweatshirt he wore when we first met, or the story he related about trying to learn to skate with his cousin the first week they arrived in Canada. Because, of course, for him, hockey was synonymous with *Canadian*. Newly arrived from Egypt at age thirteen, he recalls fervently wanting to fit into his predominantly white middle school where hockey was a big deal. He tried skating, but never really mastered it, and his family had no thoughts whatsoever of putting him into an organized sport of any kind. A dream was installed in his head, though, and he knew that if he ever ended up having a son, he would play hockey.

A dream is a dream, and when our first son turned five, we decided to put him in Learn-to-Skate lessons at the local community centre. At that time, I had no idea of the hockey future my husband was envisioning for Zak. I wasn't even thinking about hockey; I just considered that learning to skate was another physical activity he could explore in tandem with the martial arts and swimming classes he also participated in. It seemed ironic. There I was, the typical Canadian with no hockey thoughts or dreams for my son, while my Middle Eastern husband, only arriving here in the land of ice and snow as a young teenager, had already planned for his son's path to NHL stardom! In retrospect, there's a certain sense to it. At local arenas and outdoor rinks, I often see excited newcomers smiling, slipping, sliding, and hanging onto the boards for dear life as they try skating on ice for the first time. For people from sunnier climates, snow and ice are such a novelty. Everyone wants to try to skate. It's such a Canadian thing to do! I always want to tie their laces up a bit tighter and hold their hand as they shuffle across that ice.

As Canadians we can sometimes take that fun for granted. I spent a good part of my life *not* celebrating all the snowy Canadian fun we can have, actually crying when it's too cold and snowy, dreading the whole winter season, dreaming of escaping and living somewhere hot and lush. I've often asked myself, "Why would anyone *want to live here?*" Through my husband, I gained a whole new perspective. His family fought long and hard to make Canada their home and he loves it. All of it. Within a few years of being together, I realized a number of things: 1) Staying in this marriage meant I would not be moving away to the fantasy tropical island I dreamt of, as my husband loved Canada too much to ever leave; 2) I'd better revise my attitude about the cold weather if I'm staying here forever; 3) Learning to drive could help me not dread the cold Canadian winters so much (so I said goodbye to waiting on the corner for buses while crying about my frozen face, took some lessons, and got my driver's license.); 4) Proper cold-weather clothing wasn't invented for nothing (hello parka, hello toque, hello Uggs); and 5) Having fun with winter activities, like snowball fights, tobogganing, and enjoying the beauty of the first—and fortieth—snowfall of the season as you sip hot cocoa, makes it all more bearable and even something to look forward to. Oh, and the rush of hockey season!

My son's start on the ice was rocky at best. Often my husband and I felt bad for making him stay on the ice when he couldn't skate. He'd spend most of the class falling down and trying to get up over and over again (talk about determination), or giving up and just lying there making snow angels on the ice. He'd always count how many times he fell. "Mom, Dad, I only fell twenty-five times today!" Once we were down to single digits for the fall count—after about a year of weekly skating lessons—we started to wonder about hockey for Zak. Or at least my husband started to wonder about it. At the end of a skating term, we found the one female instructor who wore hockey skates rather than figure skates like the rest of the teachers and asked her about the possibility of getting Zak into hockey. Was he ready? Where could we go? How does it all work? We knew absolutely nothing. The instructor, who seemed like she had dealt with confused wannabe hockey parents before, kindly told us that yes, he was ready, and directed us to check out our local youth hockey association, scribbling down a website address for us. This was a beginning!

As soon as we got home from skating that night, I jumped on my laptop and typed the website address into the search bar. Eager to learn how to register Zak for hockey, when the term would start, what the cost was ... I was thinking of it much like the skating or swimming classes he had been enrolled in. I didn't even know enough to realize that there was a hockey season and that the season had already started. Oops! It was mid-October at this point. As if that wasn't bad enough, trying to navigate the website confirmed how clueless I was. It was filled with a whole bunch of words and terms that made no sense to me. I pored over that website for days trying to absorb all I could about this foreign land of youth hockey. Local teams, levels, age divisions, rules, and coaches ... I had no idea what any of it meant. (I don't think I had ever even watched a hockey game at that point!) I later learned that most people who were clued in had registered in the spring or summer, gone to the evaluation skate, and had already been placed on a team. After a few confusing e-mails back and forth, someone at the organization found a team that had a spot for my very beginner hockey player son. Without questioning what we were in for, we registered online and were told to show up for Sunday practice later that same week.

Two

So ... This is Hockey?!

I t was the night before Zak's very first hockey practice and we needed gear! We pulled up to our local Canadian Tire because ... that's where you got hockey stuff, right? We were on our way to a family event, so my husband waited in the car to make our apologies for running late. Zak and I raced inside; for some reason I had been put in charge of figuring out what we needed. Aware that it was almost closing time, we frantically paced up and down the hockey aisle as I scanned the equipment checklist I had found on the internet. Helmet, check. Elbow pads, check. Skates, check. We already had all of that from his skating lessons. Then, the more mysterious items I had no clue about. Luckily there were pictures beside the names on the list: chest protector, shin guards, elbow pads, neck guard, gloves, and hockey pants (which are actually more like big, padded shorts). I spotted a whole kid's hockey gear kit that included a lot of the stuff we needed. Deciding that sounded easiest, I popped it into my cart. Then I tracked down a sales associate who helped us with most of the remaining gear. He knew we were newbs and advised that we'd need a water bottle with one of those long mouthpieces to fit in the helmet cage, as well as various hockey tapes. I had no idea what all these different tapes were for, but I tossed them in my shopping cart and figured I'd look up what to do with them when I got home. As we were on our way out, we passed a rack of jerseys. Feeling super hockey-smart, I realized he might need a jersey and hockey socks to go over all this gear for the first practice until he got his actual team jersey. I grabbed a plain white jersey that was on sale for ten dollars and some basic black hockey socks. We were at the cash, all lined up, when I realized we had forgotten the most important piece—a hockey stick! Back we bustled across the store, past coffee makers and auto parts, to the hockey section. I panicked a little, recalling that I had seen *a lot* of advice online about choosing the proper stick. Zak's right-handed, so we should get a right-shooting stick, yes? I almost felt smart knowing that this means the toe of the stick is curved so you can hold the stick across your body down to your right and your dominant hand can be the bottom/main shooting hand. Other than that, I just let him pick the coolest-looking one that wasn't a crazy price. He chose a black and neon green Sherwood that just happened to be on sale ... score! Back to the cash and out into the night, our car loaded up with heaps of gear to make sense of before tomorrow's early-morning practice.

I popped out of bed bright and early, 5 am. I packed Zak's bag full of all his new gear. Then over my morning coffee, I watched multiple YouTube videos about what everything was and how to put it on properly. I was hoping to appear a little less awkward than I was imagining I'd look getting him ready in a changeroom full of other, more seasoned parents and players. After a somewhat rushed breakfast, we were all out the door and on our way to Zak's very first hockey practice! His new team's home arena was in our town's big sporting complex that combines a recreation centre, complete with three ice rinks, as well as an Olympic-sized arena where semi-pro sporting events and concerts take place. We had never been to the rec arenas in this centre before; taking it all in, we wondered how we'd know which rink we needed to be in. Eventually we located a TV screen that had all the practices of the day listed with rink and dressing room assignments for the various teams. And there we were: 7:30 am—rink 2—rooms 5 and 6. Zak and I rushed to changeroom #5. No one was there. Were we in the right place? Were we that early? Oh well, we decided to start getting ready, as I knew this first attempt might take some extra time. Somehow the two of us managed to put all the pieces together and we felt pretty triumphant. Suddenly my husband rushed in and said he'd been talking to one of the assistant coaches and that practice was about to start! It was in a different rink and changeroom than we thought. We left our 'private' changeroom and rushed off down the corridor to the proper rink.

I fumbled around struggling to open the gate onto the ice, but as soon as the friendly assistant coach noticed, he skated over with a big smile and helped me propel Zak out on the ice. He was there early skating around with his son, and Zak got to join them. My husband and I pressed our faces up against the Plexiglass ready to take in this whole new experience. Our little boy who had never even watched a game and really had no idea what hockey was, was out there on the ice. How would he know what to do? He was skating about with the man and his son, and slowly more and more kids trickled in and started warming up, stretching, skating around, and playing. Soon the head coach glided out onto the ice and started organizing some skating drills across the rink. Circles, figure eights, lines ... stuff Zak had never done before. Then he spilled a bag full of pucks onto the ice—pucks went every which way, kids eagerly swooping in to scoop them up and start pushing them around the rink. They shot, they passed, they maneuvered madly around pylons and each other. There were lots of different levels here, and we noted that Zak was definitely one of the more clueless on the spectrum. Some of these kids must have started hockey a whole year or two before us (Ice Puppies or the Paperweight Division starts at just four years old), and even the ones new this season had a month of practices under their belts. Zak would have some catching up to do!

"That stick is way too big for him - it's for an adult! Get it cut to nose-level in shoes, or chin-level in skates. And he's got a right-shooter stick, but I think he's actually a left shooter. Check that out."

We got a chance to talk to the coach after practice. This rosy-cheeked, tired-looking fellow seemed like someone who started each day chain-smoking and swigging whiskey. He had been gruffly screaming commands at the kids through the whole practice and his tone didn't soften for us. He skated up off the rink as he tossed a team jersey to us, "For the game tomorrow." Game tomorrow? Whaaaaaat? He grunted, "Zak did great for his first time." Walking away briskly, still wearing skates on the rubber flooring outside the rink area, he glanced back and called out to us, "That stick is way too big for him—it's for an adult! Get it cut to nose-level in shoes, or chin-level in skates." Continuing to walk away, he added, "And he's got a right-shooter stick, but I think he's actually a left shooter. Check that out." And he was gone. Zak was struggling to get his tight helmet off while holding his too-big-for-him hockey stick. I relieved him of the stick (which did look ridiculous to me now) and helped him undo a snap at his chin as we headed back to the changeroom. I started peeling layers of tape, skates, gear, shorts and more shorts off my sweaty boy, who was smiling from ear to ear. He was laughing with another boy beside him who was standing on the bench dancing around in just his underwear. I got a chance to talk to the father of the dancing boy. I asked when and where this game the coach just told us about was, and about the right or left stick situation. He filled me in on where to find all game and practice info on a handy app called TeamSnap and went on to explain that just because he's right-handed it doesn't necessarily mean he's a right shooter. Some right-handed players go for a left-shooting stick, as you want your dominant hand at the top of the stick. There's no definite answer, and people use various sticks, so we weren't necessarily *wrong*, but if holding this right stick felt awkward to Zak, a left-shooting stick might feel more natural. Another dad a few boys down called out, "You gotta check out Pro Hockey Life!" As there seemed to be agreement all around that this was the place to go, we decided to check it out for this other stick we might need before the next game.

The Pro Hockey Life store is huge and has everything anyone could ever want for hockey. We looked through hundreds of sticks of every sort, all very expensive, trying some we were considering out in their shooting practice area. We finally decided on one that cost four times the amount of our one-day-old Canadian Tire stick and vowed never to go to this magical, but very expensive store again. As soon as we got home, Zak called on his friends who lived across the street, two brothers a little older than Zak who played lots of hockey. They came over and shared their nine-year-old expertise teaching us where to cut the new stick and showing us some cool techniques for taping it. So that's what that tape was for!

The next day was Zak's first hockey game! A very different arena than the huge, modern multi-plex we were at the day before, today we were playing an 'away' game at an older, one-rink arena. Although it was probably the closest arena to our home—practically in our backyard—we had never been there before. We read the plain red lettering on the big white barrel-shaped building ... we had arrived! We scurried in with our huge hockey bag, stick, and extra jackets we may need as spectators in tow. The arena was a mixture of retro and modern architecture, blending new glistening glass walls with vintage fifties touches. It was gorgeous—all the beauty of a heritage building over fifty years old with great modern upgrades ... curved wooden roof, modern theatre seats all around the one ice pad, and a fully licensed bar that overlooked the rink. There was no time to take it all in right then though, as we were met by the smiling assistant coach who pointed us towards the changeroom our team was to use. Thank goodness! Inside changeroom #2 ... a party: AC/DC blasting, half-dressed kids dancing around, coaches and parents yelling back and forth excitedly! I helped Zak get geared up and left to join my husband upstairs to watch the game.

The Zamboni whirred along making its rounds, polishing the ice surface to a perfect sparkling sheet of glass for the new game. As I sipped my hot chocolate and munched nervously on arena popcorn, the two teams emerged. Uh oh ... we quickly realized we were sitting on the wrong side, the 'home' side—everyone was cheering for the home team, not ours! I looked across to the other side and recognized a few familiar hockey dad faces from the day before. I nudged my husband and said, "I think we need to be over there!" Quickly we scooted out of there and grabbed seats in the visitors' section. Both teams were scattered all over the arena taking warm-up shots on their own goalies. I searched through all the maroon jersey-wearing kids to find my son. A difficult task, as all the players looked the same in their matching uniforms and black helmets. Luckily Zak had blue skate laces, so that helped. I also know his jersey number is twelve, so that was good if I needed to identify him from the back; surnames would soon be sewn onto the back of their jerseys, but this hadn't happened yet. The game began, excitement was high! Kids were skating hard, trying to shoot at the net, coaches pointing and screaming, parents were shouting even more: "Two hands on the stick!", "Get in front of the net!", "C'mon!", "Pass it!", "Shoot!" I sat quietly, taking it all in, marveling at how well Zak was doing playing an actual hockey game for the first time. Second period came along, and the goalies changed nets. My little rookie didn't realize this and was shooting towards *his* net, now thinking he was doing great. My husband became one of the screaming parents then, jumping up, trying to get Zak's attention. "You have to shoot the other way now!", "Shoot that way!" all accompanied by wildly pointing gestures.

Zak's hockey life soon became a family affair. Both my husband and I, plus our new baby boy, would show up together for all practices and games. We noticed that usually just the dad, or sometimes just the mom, would accompany Zak's teammates to these weekly activities. What we did, I think, may have seemed odd to others. Never mind, we found it fun and exciting to watch Zak grow as a hockey player, and we were learning more and more about the game right along with him. We heard stories about other parents having a coin toss, with the loser being responsible for delivering the child to early morning hockey practice ... or families where one parent would stay home with siblings while the other took their son or daughter to the rink. Out of necessity some families with multiple kids in hockey had to juggle the two or three kids' hockey schedules between them, taxiing them to various arenas. Mostly it was the dads who brought their kids to hockey, and at the start I often found myself sitting or standing alone watching while a bunch of the dads waved my husband over to join their huddle where they'd discuss the previous night's Leafs game or how that day's ref wasn't calling any offsides. Often he would get a "hi" from the other dads, while I would be ignored. I tried not to feel excluded from this boys' club. Were we back in the fifties? My man would make his way back to sit with me and we'd laugh about it all, but I guess there was a part of him that wanted into the hockey-dad club too. As time went on and we were entrenched in our second season of hockey, I met more and more hockey moms—and some friendlier dads—and started to feel more a part of this insiders' group.

We had always heard that being involved in hockey took so much time and was so expensive. But still being green, we thought, "This isn't so bad." Time commitment: two hours a week. We had bought Zak the starter pack of hockey gear, two hockey sticks now, and paid the league for the season, equaling about a hundred dollars a month—less than what we had paid monthly for his Tae Kwon Do membership. The biggest expense was equipment, and even that wasn't horrendous. But then, about halfway into our season, we began overhearing other parents whispering about power skating Monday nights, extra practices, Saturday mornings, special clinics across town, and private shooting clinics. It seemed like a bit of a secret society, and here we were not quite knowing all the ins and outs. But thanks to a few of the friendlier awesome hockey moms and dads, we learned. And as we got to know the other parents better, our schedule got busier and busier, with extra tutorials and activities—it was the only way to improve and fast-track our son's progress, right? And suddenly we were one of those families I had sworn we wouldn't become, with our seven-year-old busy doing hockey stuff six days a week. Oh, it was fun for the most part. Not being able to party Saturday night because we had to get up early for practice wasn't that much fun. But who am I kidding? We still partied Saturday ... we'd just regret it Sunday morning as we packed up early to get to the arena! Cheering on the team together at games and looking forward to trading news and gossip as we sat through practices was a bonding experience. Zak grew to be great pals with a few of the kids on his team, and we were even starting to make a few hockey parent friends, all hanging out together at hockey, after hockey, even on days we didn't have hockey. It was an instant new social life for all of us!

Zak's second season of hockey was a little more typical, as we knew more that time around. We signed up as soon as our association opened registration in the spring. September saw Zak attending two days of evaluations to see what level team he belonged on. House league—the 'recreational' division of youth hockey—is subdivided into various levels, called different things by area. In our town there's green: total beginner, blue: that's where Zak played his first year, as he knew how to skate, but had never played hockey before, white, red, and sometimes gold. Everyone from one association/team comes out to the house league evaluations where they're taken through skating, passing, and shooting drills, sometimes play a little scrimmage, and are then assigned to the most suitable level and team. Teams play against other teams at the same level. Zak was assigned blue level again, and at the first practice, when we noticed the absence of a few of his buddies who were kind of stand-outs last season, we realized they must have moved up a level. Two older men shared the main coaching position, guys who reminded me of those two hecklers on *The Muppets*. Usually subdued and even-tempered, they could often irritate each other, resulting in loud arguments and one or the other storming off in the middle of a practice or game. Zak had fun and continued developing as a player during scheduled games and especially at his extra weekly power skating classes. It was at these sessions that my husband met up with a couple of dads whose kids were on Zak's team the year before and had moved up. He learned that they not only had moved up a level or two but had actually been asked to be on a rep team, A level.

Rep hockey is serious. Usually it's way more expensive, lots more tournaments to take part in, and just generally requires more than double the time commitment for practices and games. I've heard some families pray their kids *never* want to go beyond house league for these reasons, but rep hockey—A, AA, and AAA—sounded super exciting to us. One of the dads texted us the name of a private skating coach that the boys had been taking classes from and we decided, why not try? We also heard about 'Just Shoot It', where they work solely on your shots on a small ice pad. We did it all. It must've done something because nearing the end of the season, one of our hockey dad friends made a recommendation, and suddenly Zak was being called up all the way from blue level to sub when someone couldn't make it for an A-level game. Rep hockey is a whole other world. Rep players all carry a fancy garment bag with a freshly ironed jersey inside. Rep players often bring along two identical hockey sticks just in case one breaks or gets damaged during a game. Some players insist on having their skates sharpened at the arena a few minutes before each game. Others are picky about who sharpens their skates so they can't just get them done at any arena; I'd often hear something like, "Oh no, only Mike at Duke's can sharpen my Liam's skates." And these boys didn't have wheels on their hockey bags ... Why? Maybe they felt it was a sign of strength or toughness to be seen hoisting those huge hockey bags over their shoulders. Oh man, we were still crumpling up our sweaty jersey in a roll-y hockey bag and sharpening our skates every now and then at good old Canadian Tire.

Near the end of the season, Zak was invited out to a few skates with the A team. At the time we didn't really know what this all meant. We were happy for him to have a little more ice time and enjoy some fun with his buddies from the year before, while we got to chat with our old hockey-parent friends in the stands as we watched. Looking back, I see that these were basically try-outs before the real try-outs (that we now know mean almost nothing!) When the - *actual* try-outs came around in the spring, Zak was invited, and he was offered a spot on the A team the next day. That was, if he was willing to play defense. Now defense—or 'D'—is usually somewhat less desirable to many little boys who all want to score and be the star of the game. Defense takes a very specific type of personality, and it's not typical for most eight-year-old boys. Zak had only played forward until now, but this team needed someone to play defense and Zak didn't care—he had just made an A team! Zak signed an official card promising not to make any deals with other teams. We drove home triumphant, truly excited about what being on this new team would mean!

Three

Rep

Zak's new team started practising early, throughout the summer, way before the start of the season. The idea was to get the players working together, improving, and ready to do better that season, as we had heard they hadn't done so well the year before. Zak reunited with his old pals and instantly made many new friends. The team bonded quickly—they'd dance around and prank each other in the changeroom, play manhunt around the arena forever after practises, and even catch a movie or hockey game together away from the arena. As for the parents, it was crazy fun to magically have our social circle expanded by about forty new likeminded souls! It's bound to happen when you're thrown together with a bunch of other hockey parents, all in the same boat, four or more times a week. United in the stands screaming encouragements to our kids on the ice, pulling our hair out when our team missed an obvious shot on an open net, yelling obscenities at the refs when they did or didn't call penalties, being super-obnoxious with our clangy cowbells and noisy horns, and arguing with the parents from the other teams every chance that came along ... yep, that was us! Travelling together and spending whole weekends eating, shopping, and relaxing with each other through tournament junkets. Sharing coffee duties at super early morning practices. Seeing each other at all stages, usually fairly undone, having just stumbled out of bed. Being with hockey moms is totally different than hanging around other mom types ... We were totally used to seeing each other with no makeup, bed-head hair, almost-pyjama outfits, and of course huge, down-filled coats and the mandatory hockey mom footwear of choice, Uggs. There's a certain awesome familiarity and closeness that develops in this unique circumstance. It was something new for me and I loved it!

One of our first casual conversations with the coach of this team ran along the same lines of what we'd heard so many times in the hockey world: our town's 'demographic' was rapidly changing (which is what old white hockey people say to mean our town is getting a lot less white), which was causing hockey to die out because these newcomers somehow weren't so into the sport as the old Canadians. I heard it often ... hockey people blaming immigrants for the decline of youth hockey. Though I hadn't yet said it out loud, I wondered to myself every time, "*Why* do you think newcomers aren't so into hockey??" Maybe because of the way you higher-ups talk to and act towards newcomers whenever they try to do hockey stuff. You've got to be awfully determined to make it through all the garbage to stay in hockey as a non-white-looking person. The coach continued saying to my husband, "These new Canadians discover an old hockey puck in their garage," he makes a dumb-looking face, "and think, what's this?" I don't know why, but my husband laughed along. Once the coach was out of earshot, my husband turned to me, half-shrugged, and whispered, "What do you think he thinks I am?"

The season started, and right away we found ourselves getting ready for our first away tournament! There had been minor drama between a few parents and a team manager, but it hadn't dampened anyone's enthusiasm or excitement about this tournament weekend. Big plans for partying, drinking, watching the Leafs game on a big screen, swimming, shopping, eating out ... oh, and of course playing in a hockey tournament too. The parents almost seemed more stoked than the kids. We heard stories of who got drunk and didn't remember dancing on a table at an away tourney last season and how the kids almost got them kicked out of the hotel for playing mini stick hockey in the hall till 3 am. Friday morning, we grabbed some Timbits and coffee and started the two-hour drive out of town. Hockey kids get to miss school lots of Fridays to accommodate the tournament schedule. Until then, we had only ever done home tournaments, so the whole away-tournament experience was something new for us!

We had been told that on arrival we'd all meet in the lobby of the host hotel, check in, and then have lunch together where reservations had been made in advance at a nearby restaurant. Checking in was exciting—who doesn't love swooping into a sparkly hotel, the smell of chlorine from the pool hitting hard, getting to your room, throwing down your bags, and sprawling out on the crisp white bed? For me, this was interrupted by my two boys giddily jumping up and down on that same bed and almost bouncing on my head—that cut my fantasy-moment short. Text alerts started coming in strong on my phone as well as my husband's, then there was a knock at the door. Boisterous hockey kids announced that we were already late for lunch—let's go! I just wanted to hang out in the hotel room and order in, but we hurried off to the team lunch. We threw the hockey bag and stick in the car and made it to the restaurant in record time. It wasn't hard to find our group, taking up most of the restaurant—there was a table of all the dads, a table of all the moms, and a big rowdy table where all our offspring were ready to party (uh, *eat*). We dropped Zak off at the team table, and I said goodbye to my husband as we segregated. I squeezed myself into a seat at the mom table between two of the women I talked to most. They were all discussing the shopping they had done on the way up, joking around, giggling, and drinking: it was a party! I felt at home—I was actually loving being a part of the mom crew. As much as I used to find the segregation of genders and being split up from my husband weird when we first started hockey, I now had so many fun awesome hockey mom friends. It seemed natural, comfortable ... being able to hang with the girls, joke about the men, enjoy mom talk, etc. Being at the mom table would've been a lot more fun for me if I hadn't been the only mom with a little one—my two-year-old was on my lap screaming, fussing, and needing me to feed him. I was barely through half my grilled veggie wrap when we needed to call for the checks if we were going to make it to the arena on time for our first game. I locked eyes with my husband at the good ol' boys' table and then glanced over at the all-kids table. I saw my son and some of his friends eating multiple desserts each, including gigantic sundae creations that they would never finish. Beside the desserts were half-eaten entrees and appetizers and a slew of mega-sized pops with no more than one or two sips taken out of them. Leaving the kids on their own to order had seemed like a fun idea, that is ... until we saw this mess and waste ... and then got the bill! All the other parents seemed to think the scene was just funny; I was a little irritated and felt it was awfully indulgent (and brat-making ...?)

At the arena, the first game went well, and we were giddy with a win! We rushed back to the hotel, stopping at a few stores on our way to pick up snacks and drinks for the hockey-watching pizza party that had been arranged in the hotel conference room. I got dressed, feeling almost excited about the party. We headed down to the hotel party room ... we seemed to be the last to arrive (again). Kids were running all over, the Leafs game was on the big screen, there was a huge bucket of beer, twenty boxes of pizza, and everyone was having fun. Before I even finished my first slice of pizza, the boys had concocted a plan of going swimming *right now*! I heard a few kids ask their moms if they could go swimming just as the night had started and I thought, "Okay ladies, we need to stick together—just say no! Let's enjoy the pizza, the game, the beer for a bit here! We have the whole weekend to go swimming!" But to my surprise, everyone was saying yes! What was I to do? Be the only mom to say no? So, change of plans, all moms were now expected to go police a bunch of rowdy boys in the pool, instead of chilling at the pizza party. Whhhaat?? I told my husband to have fun for me at the now all-men's party, and I reluctantly headed back up to the hotel room so my boys could change into their swim trunks. The pool session ended up being fun, just hanging out in a hot sweaty indoor pool with the moms on patio loungers, coolers in hand, taking turns shouting at our sons to stop holding their breath under water or splashing the older gentleman trying to swim laps. But I did miss the pizza and watching the Leafs.

We had a super-early morning game the next day. After everyone stumbled out of bed and congregated for complimentary coffee in the lobby, we were off to a different arena in this small Ontario town. Zak and my husband rushed off to find what changeroom the team was in, leaving me and my younger son, Jad, to find something to do for the forty-five minutes until game time. We usually checked out the arena, ran up and down some bleachers, tried the elevator many times, admired some Zambonis, and stocked up on junk from the vending machines and snack bar. Before we could do all that, we had to get through the main lobby, where there was a marketplace set up just for the tournament. Jad was hypnotized by every table (and honestly, so was I)—hawking everything from sparkly fidget spinners, to hand-crocheted hockey-player dolls, to pom-pommed hockey toques, and giant chocolate chip cookies bigger than Jad's head. And we needed it all!

The team went on to do not-so-great at this tournament, losing almost every game. Aside from all the fun outside of hockey—the planned dining, shopping, and partying—everyone seemed ready to point fingers at whose fault it was for being up against better teams, not being well-enough prepared ... I heard it all. I can't imagine being a hockey coach or manager and hearing all the free 'advice' from hockey parents: "We should have waited to do a later tournament", "A different tournament would have been better for us", "All the teams here are a much higher level than us", "Why don't we play pump-up music and warm up like the other teams?" And on and on. No wonder our coach left the tournament halfway through to go home without so much as a word of explanation. That didn't improve matters for the team, but I think he was done with all the backseat coaching, the opinionated feedback, and all of us in general.

Back home, our team was not doing great either. We lost so many games, which made our few wins that much sweeter. The kids were developing and having fun, but the team was dead last. It was our first year on a serious rep team, so we were just happy to be there, but other parents had been serious long enough to be irritated that the team was doing so poorly.

One night, mid-season, Zak's team was up against a very tough team. They were one of the top teams and known for being rough. According to my husband, they were the worst team with the worst parents. In my head I thought, "Aren't *you* always encouraging boarding, shoving, and body checking to our son? How can you be mad at the opposing team's parents for being okay with their kids doing those same things to our players?" This is one area where I don't see eye-to-eye with my husband (or with many other hockey parents). My husband knew my stance and turned away to talk to another hockey mom who shared his sentiment about how our sons needed to get in there and use their size to dominate in the game. I'm not saying that boarding or shoving another player is never going to happen, I'm just more a fan of working on actual hockey skills rather than going with cheap shots, slides, and takedowns. On the car ride home, I pointed out how the very best and skilled players never get penalties, as opposed to the players who always seemed to be in the box causing us to be short-handed on the ice. Too often lately I had seen my son working on his physical smashes and boarding techniques more than his stick handling, deking, and passing. I asked everyone in the car, "Would you rather focus on taking someone down or making an amazing shot and scoring?" There was no answer.

"I asked everyone in the car, Would you rather focus on taking someone down or making an amazing shot and scoring? There was no answer."

One terrifying part of being in the stands is watching a player go down and not get back up. The game is bouncing along, everyone's screaming from the bleachers, lots of excitement on the rink, then you see one of the players is down. He's not getting up ... Who is it? What happened? Is it serious? So many thoughts tumble through your head. The game halts and the rest of the players go down on one knee waiting to see what will happen. A cold silence echoes through the arena. Dads try to look brave, moms usually say something like, "I can't take this shit." After a bit, sometimes the player will get up and half-skate, half-limp off the ice. Other times a coach shuffles out onto the ice to check on the injury and help the child up and over to the bench. Both teams bang their sticks on the ice and everyone in the bleachers claps to cheer on the injured player for getting up. And the game goes on. Whenever this happens, a million articles and posts I've read about that kid in Minnesota or Calgary who died or got paralyzed playing a hockey game just like this roll through my head. At tense times when someone is lying on the ice unresponsive in the deafening quiet of the cold arena, I often ask myself if it's worth the risk. "Why are we putting our son in this type of danger?" or "Why do boys always have such dangerous hobbies?" Then the kid gets up and the thought magically disappears from my mind... until the next time.

Over the past few years of attending my son's games, I've pin-pointed the most intense, interesting, and sometimes dangerous place to sit while watching. It's right in the middle, as close as you can get to the other team's crazy parents! If you're the visiting team and they're the home team, you sit in the visitors' section, but central enough that you're near the home fans. We used to do it by mistake, but now it's entertainment! You wouldn't believe what comes out of parents' mouths when 'cheering' on their kids: "Murder him, Jesse! Get him!", "What are you doing? You're killing me!", "Smash number 33! BOARD HIM!" Myself, I'm a big fan of "WOO-HOO!!!", "YAY!", or "Go Zak!" I've even seen some fights erupt between parents on opposing teams or a parent and a ref when there's a dispute about a penalty, goal, or offside call. Parents and coaches have been escorted out of arenas because of vicious arguing and threats. The screaming comes from all sides: "Pressure!", "Stay with him!", "Get Him!", "SKATE!", "Both hands on the stick", "Stick on the ice!" The funny thing I've learned along the way is that the kids usually can't hear any of it down on the ice. It's really just for us. This can infuriate some parents who think they're screaming a meaningful nugget of advice or encouragement down at their junior hockey star. When the player doesn't seem to respond, take notice, or *do* the thing, the parent proceeds to yell a little louder, repeating their 'suggestions,' perhaps emphasized with some big, dramatic gestures. They feel like the kid is blatantly ignoring all of this, but they just can't hear them down on the ice. Most seasoned hockey parents realize our kids can't hear us, but maybe yelling and calling out advice makes us feel engaged, like we're almost with our kids as they fight the good hockey fight. I've come to know all the parents on our team and their favourite phrases and shout-outs. One dad screams out in Russian "Devay Davay!", a mom mumbles some French prayers under her breath, a trio of peppy hockey moms have a clapping and screaming chant down, and when a goal goes in our net, our goalie's mom always stands up and yells "RESET!" to her son. My husband is a fan of shouting "OFFSIDE!" and "SHOOT!" in a voice that sounds nothing like the man I married. There are air horns, sirens, and cowbells. Oh, the cowbells! A mom sitting beside me in the stands once confessed, "I can't stand cowbells—I think I have PTSD from cowbells." The stands are a whole show on their own—total entertainment!

It was an awesome season full of new friendships, tons of ice time and development, victories and (lots of) losses, away tournaments, early mornings, late nights, carpooling, some drama ... and then, the end-of-season party! Fuelled by greasy pizza and way too much pop, the kids ran, danced, and jumped about in their matching team jerseys, which were way too big for them without the usual armour-like gear underneath. My husband and I hung out with some of the parents, and it was a good time all around. That is, until the coach called my husband over to talk alone in a corner over Budweisers and pretzels. I was busy with my youngest screaming at the sight of the team mascot dancing around, but I heard enough of the start of the conversation to know what he was telling him. It seemed to take my husband longer to understand the coach's tiptoeing around and hinting. We all knew it was a possibility ... Zak had skipped a lot of levels, getting into rep hockey from blue (entry-level) house league, but he had really developed over the year, and while he wasn't their strongest player, he was getting better and better all the time. The coach had kind of warned us by saying he was cutting a lot of the kids this year, but I don't think we had really lived with the reality ... until that night. Zak was cut from the team. Why a coach would think that a fun end-of-season party was the time to tell a family their ten-year-old son will not be on the team anymore is beyond me. Harsh. But that's how it happened. I left without saying goodbye to anyone. Our smiling son bounced out of there saying his goodbyes, oblivious to what had gone down. It was now our job to deliver that news. Gulp.

Later that night, my husband told me the coach had passed our name on to a coach of another A team that was looking for players and we could try that, but he strongly recommended going back to house league. How could we? House league seemed so watered down after having experienced the two-practices-plus-two-games a week in rep. Our son would have to stop all the body contact that he had become used to with rep hockey, as it isn't at all allowed in house league. And why would we want our son to be a big fish in a small pond when he could continue growing and reaching for the stars in the big sea of rep hockey? The coach had tried to convince my husband that Zak would improve if he felt like he was dominating in house league. We knew our son better, and neither of us was on board with that. We're all about growing, not being comfortable. What distinguishes a player as rep level? Mainly they become so elite because they play more than house-league players. Sure, there's raw talent sometimes too, but a lot of it is more time spent working on skills, playing games, doing the thing! Plus, knowing our personalities, we also just wanted to 'show' everyone (especially that coach) that Zak could dominate in rep hockey, thank you very much!

A few days later, a hockey mom friend called me to tell me they were in the same boat—her son had also been cut from the team in the same way we were—even worse than our party cut, if that's possible. Like me, she was hurt, angry, and confused. We semi-joked about a few theories of why we had been cut, discussed our options for other teams at this late date, laughed, and cried together. She revealed what she had found out about a secret team party that we hadn't been invited to, and how a certain parent had hinted to her about how we might all be cut. Realizing that everyone knew we had been cut at the end-of-season party and never let on was a bitter pill to swallow. I suppose they were in a difficult position and didn't know the best way to deal with it all. Touchy subject ... did they keep things to themselves because they were worried about jeopardizing their own relationship with the coach and team. Maybe I would've done the same thing, being in their position? Whatever the reasons, it left us feeling a little betrayed by some of the people we had thought of as friends.

For weeks after, opening a closet and seeing all the hoodies and hats emblazoned with the old team's logo made me sad. What do you do with all that team paraphernalia when you're done with a team and don't plan to feel fuzzy nostalgia for them again? I guess that's why second-hand shops have such a collection of old hockey jerseys and sports clothing. Part of me wanted to burn all the hockey team stuff we had acquired. But I couldn't do it. I'd be on Facebook and see all the happy pictures of the old team. I felt sad and confused ... and yes, nostalgic. We had all been like family for a year—together at least four nights a week and pretty much living with each other on weekend-away tournaments ... eating, partying, swimming, shopping, sharing the highs and lows. Now I just felt detached and shut-out from all those close relationships. Brutal.

Four

Movin' On

All A team try-outs are scheduled on the exact same day and time as one another. This means that trying out for more than one team is virtually impossible. I don't understand the logic—to me it seems crazy. Why not let everyone try out for any team they want and then decide, but I guess that would put the families and players in the power position, when that's where coaches/teams want to be. We had learned through this whole process that most of the teams are pretty much picked during the last season, and the try-outs really don't mean much; they're try-outs in name only. Too bad we were told 'way too late that we'd need to find another team, just a week or so before these try-outs. The decent thing to do would have been to let us know much earlier so we could've had a fair chance to woo coaches months before the actual try-outs that weren't really try-outs. At this late date, practically every team we talked to said they were looking to fill just *one* spot ... with anywhere from ten to thirty players competing for that sole elusive position. We quickly realized that no kid in the middle of the pack was ever going to be chosen for a team; you had to be the very best of everyone to even stand a chance. We had to consider carefully and pick which team we might have the best chance with. Zak's former coach had referred him to a team, and one of the coaches came out to see him skate at a class he was taking a few days before try-outs. When we were advised that he had potential and would be competitive at try-outs if he showed up, that helped us make our decision. Monday night we were off to their try-outs!

Since this was the lowest team in the association, we weren't expecting their try-outs to be as packed as they were. Word on the street was that the best team in the league had been cheating, using players from higher levels the season before—now that team was not returning, so all their amazing players would be trying out for other teams. Half that team was at these try-outs. Also on the ice were two ten-year-old boys, as tall as my husband, who looked like football linebackers, plus a slew of other super-keen players. The try-out went really well for Zak—we thought he rocked it. Maybe every parent thinks this? We felt we were able to be objective about our son's abilities and level; we didn't think he was always the best or perfect, but he looked great out there. We were concerned about the large number of players trying out: exactly how many spots did they need to fill? Watching a try-out, you can't help sizing up all the contenders ... They need anywhere from fourteen to seventeen players for a team. Okay, everyone in the red helmets were on the team last year, so they were all going to make it—that's ten spots right there. We studied the other fifteen, all in various team colours from their previous teams. Two awesome stand-out forward players, two massive guys the coaches kept pointing at that I guessed they were considering for defense, a few who weren't the very best but were far from the worst, and then there were a few who glaringly didn't fit in skill-wise—maybe just there to practise and have a skate. Back in the changeroom, my husband heard one of the team dads mention that a lot of their players were trying out for other teams tonight, but that they'd be back for day two of try-outs. And just like that, my counting-and-elimination theory was out the window.

The next day my husband got a call from the coach. After hemming and hawing a bit, saying things like at that point Zak was on the outside looking in, and that he was expecting a lot of his players to return to the team ... he told us we were welcome to come to the second day of try-outs if we wanted to—but that it wasn't looking so great for us. My husband asked if he thought Zak had a chance, and the coach said, "You never know; but if I had to say now, I'd probably say no." My husband came home from work super early and we were bummed together. Then we jumped into action, going into full-on sports agent mode. We began e-mailing and calling every A team that might want to see our son. We started branching out to other areas ... how far were we willing to go four days a week? We decided we would consider some nearby associations that played further afield and started contacting the teams to find out if there was a try-out or skate we could attend. We ended up trying out for different teams every single day that week and having very similar experiences at each. There was usually only one spot available with a bunch of kids vying for it, so unless you were THE ONE they were noticing, it was over almost before it began. We had a few near wins, but it always came down to "There was someone better than your son." This was taking a toll on my husband, who was getting progressively more stressed/angry/down about it. He told me he wasn't really working much, couldn't focus at the gym, didn't want to eat. All his energy was on how we were going to get Zak on a rep team. WHAT HAD HAPPENED TO US? Was this what being a hockey parent was all about? We were getting desperate and started to feel defeated. Zak didn't seem to share our stress. He was a champ doing skate after skate, try-out after try-out, and not seeming too bothered by any of it. As we shivered through watching one look-see, a dad told us he didn't even let his son know he was going to a try-out because he didn't want to stress him out—he would just tell him it was a skate to get in some practice. Oops, we weren't even thinking about that (well, until he brought it up). Had we been so focused on finding a team for Zak that we never even wondered how the endless try-outs were affecting him? I stopped to think about how that might be impacting him and even asked him about it. He seemed fine and said he was also eager to find a new team. I had noticed that he was growing and improving the more he tried out for different teams and met various types of coaches and players along the way. We thought about what we would do if no rep team offered him a spot. What house league was our best bet to get called up to their A team in the season? The one thing we all agreed on was that we were NOT going back to our old association.

We came away from this painful experience learning a lot. 1) Zak needed to *kill it* on the ice. He couldn't get lazy. We saw so much more from him through the try-out week when the pressure was on than we did through the whole last season. 2) We needed to invest in some double A and high-level training with influential trainers for him. And 3) As parents, we needed to be more social, have an ear out more ... 'play the game'. So, forget sitting together as a family—we'd have to think about doing what most people do: men sit with the men, women gossip with the women. We needed to get in there. It's so much politics, it's so much about who you know, who likes you, and what alliances you've formed. We saw this clearly multiple times. At our last try at A teams, we showed up for a power skating session where the coach said he'd have a look at us, as he had that one more spot left on his team. A boy who had played with Zak in the past was now on this team and was also at this class. We were getting geared up, and when his dad saw us in the changeroom, he looked like he had seen a ghost. I didn't know why—why would he care that we were trying out for the team? His son had already secured a spot. Why wouldn't he be happy to see us and potentially have us on the team with them? The dad sat with the coach laughing and talking through the whole session, a few rows behind us. He acted as if he didn't know us at all when he was with the coach. I wanted to turn around to see if the coach was even looking at what was happening on the ice. Did he even *see* that impressive shot my son just made, or was he being kept too busy laughing with this dad we used to be pals with? Lessons, lessons...

Everyone had been so guarded and secretive about what they were doing all season. I hadn't realized it at the time, but saw now that it had all been part of a game we hadn't yet learned the rules of. A bunch of families had decided to find other teams and had coaches come and scout their sons through the season, but none of us knew ... well, at least *we* didn't know. I had thought I was kind of close to some of the moms, but I didn't know anything about their strategies and secret moves until it was way too late.

We had signed up to play three-on-three hockey with players from the old team throughout the summer, and now we were wondering if we should just not bother. We felt out of the group. If it had been up to my husband, we probably would've dropped out, but my son was still tight friends with all the boys from his previous team, and I thought we should go ahead with our plan. The first few weeks my husband refused to show his face and talk to all our old hockey-parent friends, so I took Zak solo, and that was weird. People totally noticed: "Wow, we've never seen you without your other son and husband!" The first day was a little awkward. I guess no one knew what to say to us now that the whole truth was out: Zak wouldn't be returning to the team next year. Quickly it improved, though, and parents were actually very nice to me in the end. Three-on-three went great. Zak had developed so much because of all the stress of being forced to up his game through all those crazy try-outs (which everyone noticed and commented on). And nothing had changed between the boys. They still delayed getting into their gear because they were busy shooting the puck around the changeroom, did Fortnite dances when they scored on the ice, and noisily discussed their upcoming trip together to Canada's Wonderland. Impromptu basketball games outside the arena after hockey made us think we should bring some wine and have a parents' parking lot party every week!

Around the start of summer, we got an offer for Zak to join a red-level team (top of the rec level, but not quite rep—a step down) with our old association. Yes, the same association we had vowed never to join again. The new coach seemed enthusiastic and like he was really trying to build a solid team and take it as seriously as any rec-level team. So, a tad reluctantly, we accepted the offer. Zak would play a guaranteed forward position for this new team. We had a few semi-offers to play defense on some far-away rep teams, but no luck trying to grab a forward spot. Zak had accepted a defense position on his A team the year before just to get in, but playing forward was his clear preference. I could see the previous season that he'd wanted to play forward so badly that he stopped being excited about the defense position. He was motivated and aggressive when playing forward, but the spark just wasn't there when he played defense. Most boys want to be the big hero centre position of course, so it's a lot harder to get a forward position on rep teams. You can often find defense positions (especially if your son is on the taller side), but forward can be tough, especially late in the game. We asked Zak if he would take a defense position to get on a rep team, and the answer was always no. Teams would often say stay open-minded, try defense, you could move to forward mid-season. But Zak had tried defense for a whole year; the few times he got to play forward showed us all that that was where he really wanted to be. Even if it meant going down a level to do that.

The first few months on this new team felt a little awkward for me, my husband, and our son. A lot of these people had been on a different team together for years before moving here, everyone seemed to be friends, there were established nicknames, and all the boys were tight, joking and laughing together in the changeroom. My normally very social son looked alone and bummed, so I pointed him to a few other boys who were also new to the team and in the same situation as he was ... maybe he could try sitting by them and striking up a conversation? That seemed to get the ball rolling. I did the same, trying to share pleasantries with the moms who were new like me. No one was particularly unfriendly; it just wasn't like last year. My husband never wanted to go into the changeroom to help with skate-tying. I became the total hockey mom, taping socks and tying laces, which was new to me, as that had always been my husband's job in the past. Being in and around the changeroom pre-game opened up my perspective ... AC/DC blasting, half-dressed sweaty boys shouting, coaches yelling their pre-game notes over them, hockey dads (and maybe a few moms) discussing Mitch Marner's amazing goal the night before. These boys were at the age where they really should have been tying their own laces, they were almost starting to look like teenagers, and at eleven years old, some were already taller than their parents, but most still wanted mommy or daddy to tie those skates up tight enough before a big game. Some people might consider that indulgent of us or childish of them, but for me it seemed like maybe it was the last year my son would need or want me for something like this. I could feel we were coming to the end of an era. I knew he *could* tie his own laces, he had done it before, but they'd always be a little too loose. Of course it would all come with practice, and he wouldn't have mommy tying his laces forever, but for now I had the magic touch—taping his hockey socks just right and tying his skates tight enough, but not too tight. The main coach was friendly, always hugging and cheery, so that helped us feel welcome, but we were really missing our tribe from the previous year's team. We had become such a tight-knit group, like a family in a way... you didn't always agree or like what someone was doing, but like a family, you always loved each other deep-down and were together. One day, walking into our home arena for an extra practice on a holiday Sunday (there was free ice so our coaches took advantage!), we ran into our team from the year before, who were just finishing their practice and leaving as we arrived. There were many warm hugs and much excited chatting as we reunited in the lobby of the arena where we had spent so much time bonding. The boys were high-fiving, laughing, and catching up while their parents did the same. Out of the corner of my eye I could see the coach who had cut us from the team at the end-of-year party; I wasn't surprised he didn't come over to say hi. It was so fun catching up with some of the moms I hadn't seen in ages ... laughing, gossiping, and promising to arrange get-togethers for the boys soon.

There comes a point every year when a team really bonds. Sometimes it just takes time; often it's after spending a whole weekend together at a tournament, sometimes it's a particularly stressful situation or drama, this time maybe it was the holidays? The first game back after the Christmas holidays with our new team, we were going up against the toughest team, a team that had beaten us badly the previous time we had played them. Sitting in the bleachers at the start of the game just felt different. Something had clicked with our team; we were sitting together, closer than usual, joking about stuff, trying to stay positive about this tough game that was about to begin. There's a moment when your team scores (especially in a tough game) where I think everyone tears up a little with happiness and pride even if it's not your child who scored. I love this about being a team! We were finally at that sweet spot where we knew all the players' first names as opposed to just the last name they wear on their jersey. We even knew what number some kids were and could now scream out "GO MIKEY!" and "GOOD ONE, ADAM!" rather than random general cheers. It was a very close game, nearly a tie, but we ended up losing 3 – 4. It almost felt like a win, as the last time we had played this team they killed us, winning 5 – 1. Parents often say things like "If only we had got one more shot on net," or "We really could've won that game" ... and then I think to myself, if we could've, why didn't we? It's just like when we get in the car after a game and my son and husband start discussing how he *could've* scored five times that game ... I hate to be the negative one, and I guess coming close to scoring is a step in the right direction, but in the end he didn't score, right? We needed to work on shots. It always came down to this. My son would discuss how awesome a skater he is, how great his edgework and backwards crossovers are, how he sets up plays. I always tried to figure out a good way to bring him back to reality without weakening his confidence ... What about scoring though? The year before he had played defense, so there was less emphasis on scoring, but now that he was getting his chance to play winger and sometimes centre, he needed to prove he could not only skate great, but also actually *score!* When we contemplated asking some higher-level coaches to come out to watch him play in hopes of getting back on a rep team the next year, we were worried that he wouldn't stand out as a strong enough forward at that point. Because shooting and scoring certainly makes people take notice!

I was frustrated trying to understand why my husband was being so lazy about hockey that year. We had missed so many practices and even games because Zak was feeling a bit unwell or we were out late the night before ... things that would never have kept us from hockey the year before. The whole team was excited about our first out-of-town tournament ... except my husband. He just didn't seem to care about driving out of town and staying over the weekend. What? We *had* to do the tournament! We were going to miss out on everything ... if he thought we hadn't bonded with the team yet, we really wouldn't if we missed this opportunity. Why didn't he want to be a part of this? I tried to tell him how excited everyone had been in the changeroom about partying Friday night, all the fun we were going to have, the hotel, the drive up, everything! He still wasn't sold. And Zak seemed ... indifferent. I started wondering why *I* cared so much then, and I decided to let it go. I didn't book the hotel, we decided to drive up to play the games and then return home every night. Everyone else seemed okay with missing out on all the weekend team fun. I just didn't get it, but that was the plan. The crazy thing about this tournament? Everyone drove up to a small Ontario town about an hour and a half away from where we lived ... and we played against five other teams from *our* town. Who also had to make that trip. Why didn't we just all stay home and play? It was a bit comical.

A little later into the season, our coach sent out a message asking if anyone was interested in trying to move to A next year—the team we had been on the year before. Wouldn't everyone want to? How many people were they looking for? Was there a new coach? (We had heard the coach who cut us the year before had left mid-season). So many questions... We talked briefly to our coach after the game and he seemed to think Zak would be a great fit—the team was not doing well, a lot of our favourite people on that team were probably leaving for other teams, and did we even want to be on that team? Zak got called up to play with them a few times. He played hard, we met the new coach, and we reunited with our old hockey friends in the stands and got brought up to date on all the team gossip.

The year before we learned (too late) that the official advertised try-outs for rep teams in the spring really don't mean much; anyone thinking about moving up a level or switching teams throws on their big-time agent hat for their eleven-year-olds at the start of the new year, while still waist deep in the current season and about to go into playoffs. That year, we vowed to learn from our naïve hockey-parent experience and start contacting prospective coaches earlier, going to skates, and having coaches come and watch games. We started hunting down all the coaches we needed to contact. We searched team websites for contact info, and when that didn't work, we became stalkers tracking down rep coaches on Facebook, LinkedIn, Instagram, Twitter, wherever we could get the info. I wrote everyone at the start of the new year and waited a week or two. I didn't get many responses other than some questions about where he played, position, etc. ... and we started wondering if that was really how it was done. Did they expect people to send a press release? A demo video? Whaaaat? Just as I was ready to start splicing together Zak's greatest hockey moments complete with F/X and set it to a fitting song like 'Eye of the Tiger,' online research told me NO, I should definitely not do that!

A few weeks later the skate invites started pouring in. One Saturday we had two skates on either side of a game with our current team. We left the house at 7 am. The second skate of the day was at an arena we'd never been to in Toronto. Toronto arenas are so very different from our town's usual arenas. They're older, a little creepier, have a little more character—they're interesting, almost like we're at an away tournament in Buffalo or something. Walking into this foreign arena, we were surprised to be greeted by cheery, familiar faces. A few parents from the team we were on the previous year were there with their kids for the same try-out. There was a mix of "Oh, you're here too! Yay!" and

"Oh, *you're* here too! Why?" The boys got to chat while tying their skates, and we reconnected with our old hockey friends while watching our kids fight for that one spot on the team.

"You really bond with other hockey parents through how crazed you've all become."

You really bond with other hockey parents through how crazed you've all become. There must be some parents who can remain calm and don't become obsessed, spending every waking minute of their lives at the rink for the latest shooting clinic, try-out camp, and drills class. But truthfully, I haven't met them yet. Then there's us … discussing the latest skate-sharpening technique and the *only* place to get it done, or the secret power skating class our children *need*. Sharing secrets (but not too much) … we weren't telling each other our next move or what skate/look-see we'd be at the next morning—even when we were out drinking together the night before! We left that as a surprise when we met at the arena the next day and our boys were up against each other fighting for that one coveted spot on the second-best team in the town next to ours.

Obviously, I had a small handful of hockey-parent friends who I shared everything with—highs, lows, and hockey opportunities for our kids. If there was a spot on our team opening up and they were looking, we'd recommend them and vice versa. But the rest of my hockey-parent 'friends' confused me. Maybe it was because I've never been good at holding back and compartmentalizing. You're friends, but you don't share *everything* with some of these friends? Frenemies at times? I have an issue not totally letting my guard down, but I've learned you can't do that as a hockey parent; you need to keep some things to yourself. I'm usually an open book, but suddenly you find another hockey mom sitting next to you at a try-out where both your boys are vying for the same position, as there is only one coveted spot available ... It can be dicey. That 'last man standing' thinking takes hold: are you friends at that point? It can be confusing. This happened to me several times, and I wasn't sure what the protocol was. It was like we were in this together, but we were not. Like that awkward moment when you sit on the wrong side of the rink at a game or even near the middle and end up right beside a rival team's family shouting to kill someone on your team, maybe even your son!

Aaaaand the skates continued. There I was in my usual spot, awkwardly waiting outside the changeroom with all the other keener parents trying to figure out which one of these coachy-looking men bustling by was the one I had been e-mailing back and forth about trying out for his team. Why didn't anyone ever introduce themselves to us all and tell us how it was going to go down at the start (or ever) so we wouldn't have to be awkward and confused? I saw big teenagers going on the ice ... Was I even at the right place for this skate? Was this a class? Was this a quasi team practice? Would they tell us what to do or where to go? Should I tell someone about Zak so they knew to watch him out there? It was always the same. I still hadn't figured out what was what, but all of a sudden everyone was on the ice, so I rushed Zak out to the side of the ice where players looked about his age and hoped for the best. I heard people talking about this being for 2007s (we were 2008), and I also realized there were two people splitting the ice and that's why there was such a mix of ages. This was a tough one—I was assuming two levels up from what he was playing and maybe a year older? But really, who knew? The skate was coming to an end, and I was dreading going back and waiting around for something to happen or someone to say something about ... anything. I always thought my husband should have been the one repping Zak, as he's more social and extroverted in these circumstances. And he's a dude, which is the norm for who usually chats up the coaches about their son. This season, though, that responsibility had fallen to me because I'm the "white, Canadian-looking parent." As much as I didn't want to believe that coaches may operate from racist biases, the previous year's try-outs had convinced my husband that they didn't respond as well to his Arabic look as they did to my white-bread Canadian-ness. So far I hadn't noticed a big advantage, and I wondered if being beige or a woman was worse to these coaches. So, once again, I waited awkwardly outside the changeroom with a bunch of parents I didn't know, wondering if someone was going to say something to me or if I should say something to someone. Where was the coach I needed to speak to? What did this skate cost? Who did I need to pay? Did anyone even know what we were doing there?

My husband waited in the car outside and was full of questions I didn't have answers to. We had actually argued several times about this. Suddenly I remembered how try-outs magically transformed my husband into an even crazier hockey dad than he usually was. Yes, I'm a committed hockey mom, but nothing like him—try-out drama doesn't keep me up at night, it doesn't ruin my entire day, week, or month like it can for him.

Being a hockey mom looking for a rep team for your child to play on is like being a desperate, single, middle-aged woman searching for 'the ONE.' You have your first date (first invited skate), might have a second date (initial try-out), then you just never hear from them again. Do you follow up? Keep hounding them? Ask pointed questions like, "Should we come to another skate?" or "Did you like what you saw?" Or ... do you just let it go, understanding that they weren't that impressed, or they would've committed by now? You see parents whose kids get places because of their pushy advocating. Kids who aren't as skilled as your child are on teams ... and they're not even the coach's kid. I have to question whether I could have been more proactive, more persistent ... Was I not *doing* enough?

It was the big night—the final try-outs; every team at the same time—and our last chance to figure out where we would put our hopes and energies. Each family had to pick which team they thought would be best, which team might offer them a spot, which team or teams might not even be *around* next season. We had already heard that three of the eight teams might be folding, as they didn't have enough kids registered for that age/level. We had talked in advance to some of the coaches, shown up for various pre-try-out skates, but as usual, coaches had excelled at stringing us along, saying things like they *may* have *one* forward spot and they needed to wait till try-outs to see. After lots of family deliberation, we finally decided on the one team we hadn't had any issues with yet ... and we had heard they may have a few openings ...

Parents seemed on edge, their nerves only half-hidden. A lot was riding on this. Watching the try-out, we chatted with an old team manager friend and a double-A coach Zak had been practising with recently; as we watched the action on the ice, we discussed all of our kid's chances here, we heard news of another team that had a not-so-great turnout for their try-outs that night (should we be there instead?), and we texted another coach to see if we should boot across town to his team's try-out as soon as this one ended. Afterwards we all stalled in the lobby, waiting to see if anyone was going to tell us anything. Would anyone be called over to a huddle with the head coach in a corner, whispering about this one or that one's future with the team? All that happened was one of the coaches falling all over himself chasing the AA player who was dropping down to A this year. He cornered the player and his mom and very enthusiastically pointed out that they should sign with his team as all the waiting hopefuls looked on. Another coach dismissively waved the rest of us away, calling back, "Second day of try-outs Sunday. See you all then!"

So now we had a day to wait. To wonder. To let the annoyance with all the indecision and stringing along fester. To torment ourselves with second-guessing our decision about which team to go for ... and many what-ifs. We felt the need to stay busy, to distract ourselves. We called other coaches. We confirmed with the team we had tried out for that they wouldn't be making any offers until after the second day of try-outs (except of course for the lucky few who we had heard through the grapevine had already been signed). We had wild notions of trying to start our own team. We concocted a plan to send a spy to an arena to survey the competition on a team we were interested in but couldn't make the try-out for because we'd be across town at this other try-out. Somehow we got through the day and the next day's try-out.

In the end, we didn't make any of the teams we tried out for. We did get a few offers of defense only, one team we tried out for folded, one coach told us our son was too tall (whaaaaat?), plus, a whole lot of other conversations and drama. Then, when we thought it was all over, out of nowhere we ended up at a skate for a rep team one year older ... and just like that, Zak was invited to start on the team the very next day!

It was amazing to see how much talent these kids had — they were shining superstars to us! My son, who had known nothing about hockey just a few years ago, had become a solid, strong player; an absolute pro in my eyes. That was a huge inspiration to me. Seeing him progress so quickly, being super impressed by his skating and hockey brain was having an effect on me, although it took me a while to realize. I loved this hockey thing! Maybe if he could do it, I could too? I didn't totally believe this ... but I was ready to try!

Five

I Touched the Puck!

To me, hockey is the most impressive sport out there. Nothing compares to weaving around people, balancing on blades on slippery ice, with a stick, trying to get a tiny puck into a net guarded by a giant padded goalie! Goals are hard to come by, unlike scoring in a game like basketball, where players are racking up a point or two every minute. When someone scores in hockey, it seems doubly exciting and much more impressive. It's also the most challenging sport to practice. With football or soccer, you can just go out to a lawn or field with a ball and drill stuff; hockey practice requires ice time, plus being all geared up. Canadians love watching hockey, but when it comes to actually playing ... that's another matter.

The challenge of jumping in and learning as an adult, having the confidence and time commitment to keep improving—not to mention the worry of falling and breaking something—often keep grown-ups from taking a class or joining a league. Parents wanting to experience hockey life vicariously may account for so many kids being signed up for hockey regardless of whether they've expressed an interest. I think all hockey parents at some point should try lacing up themselves and playing hockey, even if it's just a couple of times. It definitely gives you perspective, as well as an appreciation for all that your junior hockey star is doing out there while you sip your hot cocoa in the stands. It might even help you bite your tongue the next time you go to bark out something like, "SKATE HARDER DAMMIT!" Because nothing beats firsthand insight into how difficult their task is out there. But the main reason I was drawn to playing myself is that I love a challenge. I love doing hard stuff. I love being a beginner at something and working hard to develop skills and knowledge in a totally new realm—that excites me! So, when I figured out from watching my son's path into the hockey world that this seemed like the hardest thing I could ever do, I was hooked. Terrified, giddy with excitement to try, but hooked.

I had skated throughout my childhood, in girly figure skates, but that had been over twenty years ago. Now I wanted to see if I remembered how. Zak was going to some family stick-and-puck times at the rink to work on moves and technique. My husband bought skates and went with him a few times as I watched with our baby from the bleachers. After several weeks, complaints that these sessions were making dad's already-bad back lots worse, was my cue to step in. What's a girl to do but strap on her hubby's oversized skates and too-tight helmet and try it out? Never having worn hockey skates, or what I always thought of as 'boy' skates before (not to mention too-big ones!), I was surprised that I could skate at all right off the bat. Stopping, though, was another matter! I would just slam into the boards ... and I may have grabbed on to my son, pulled him down and landed on him more than once. Yep, he still reminds me of this!

I remembered seeing the women's teams playing in the arena beside where Zak was playing one season. They looked hardcore. I was intrigued. I imagined what it would be like to take on the challenge of getting into something so new and foreign to me. I wondered if I could make a commitment to a team, knowing the hard work it would take to keep up and not let everyone down. Could I learn? Would I embarrass myself? What would it feel like to be all armoured up in those huge shoulder pads and funky shin guards? It happened that our across-the-way neighbours were a total hockey family, with both kids playing on teams, always being chauffeured to practices and going out of town for tournaments. Chatting with the boys one day when they were over playing with Zak, I learned that their mom also played on a hockey team. That piqued my interest immediately, and I bombarded them with questions. Pausing their game of hide-and-seek, I fired away: Where does she play? What's the name of the association? How long has she played? Has she ever been hurt playing? I couldn't stop … I was excited! Maybe she could take me with her and we could be hockey-playing besties on a team together next year. I had already canvassed all my friends, asking if they wanted to come play on a hockey team with me and was pretty much laughed at by everyone. This was it … I figured she might be my in to the hockey world. The boys did have me a little worried when they proudly told me she once got punched in the head by a player on an opposing team. Whoa, I thought, I'll have to make time to ask her about all of this in person sometime. Maybe (hopefully) the boys were exaggerating?

Apart from the obligatory "Hi, how are you?" called across the street as we were coming and going, and all the X-Box our boys played together, I really didn't know the adults in the hockey family across the street. Months later, I finally got a chance to talk with the mom. This was my opportunity, and I wasn't going to waste it.

"So, I hear you play hockey? That's so awesome! I want to play too!" There, I said it. "Where do you play? How long have you been playing? Do you think I could do it? I'm a total beginner. I heard you got punched in the head!" Everything I had been wondering about came spilling out. She looked slightly amused.

"You should definitely join a team. I've played since I was a kid, and I'm in the intermediate level on a local senior league, but I've decided not to play this season. They have a beginner level too. You could join that, you'll be fine." Aww, there went my dream of us trekking off to our hockey games together. The story I had heard about her being slammed into the boards and getting punched in the face or something like that (was I now exaggerating?) came to mind, and I wondered if that's why she decided not to play that season.

"Oh no, is it because of that person who hit you? Your kids told me about that. That's scary."

"No, no, no," she giggled, "I really haven't been hurt much at all. I mean, there was that one time when another player socked me in the head, but that was it really. Some people take themselves too seriously and think they're in the NHL," she laughed. "We're just too busy with the boys' hockey games on weekends. Sometimes my games were at 10 or 11 at night. I just want to be getting into bed at that hour." To me, late games sounded great, after the kids were in bed.

"I guess," I said, "But then you can go have a drink with your team after and it's a fun night!"

"Sounds like you need to join a beer league, Meagan!" A BEER league? What was that, and where did I sign up? In my true nerdy fashion, I made a mental note to Google that as soon as I got home.

I felt more informed and knew a lot of stuff I needed to research now. I was still stuck, though, for someone I could do this with. I think of myself as fairly independent and enjoy doing things on my own, but this seemed a little intimidating to do solo, even for me. I knew it would be a hard sell because most of my friends were into dance or Zumba or some other equally girly activity, so they would say no right away. And I figured the few friends or acquaintances who might have had a bit of interest wouldn't want to take on an activity that required a hefty-ish financial commitment for the necessary gear, equipment, and league fees. I did have one friend who had played hockey a few years earlier. Her daughter played, and her husband even taught women's hockey classes ... that seemed promising. I called her. We tried to figure out what team or classes we could join together, but she lived on the other side of the city, and we both had busy families—it was hard to get out to do anything for ourselves, never mind having to coordinate our schedules and go far from home to do it. Was there a hockey league that played somewhere between our homes at a good time for both of us that would work? We tried to figure it out but never really came up with a solution. After looking up the women's hockey league in my area, studying their website for hours, almost pressing 'register' countless times, I finally took the plunge. "Register as individual for fall season?" Yes! I did it!

A week later, there it was: an e-mail from the league organizer saying they were going to put me on a team that was missing a player, and could I play defense? It was happening! They also advised that they were having a developmental class during the week in conjunction with the Sunday night games we would play. And all starting next week! That forced a deadline. I had mere days to gather all the gear that I was missing. I had my husband's too-big skates, which were almost fine as long as I wore bulky double socks ... I had a helmet ... I even had the stick I had tried to maneuver around during my stick-and-puck forays. For all the rest, I was off to check out sales at Canadian Tire and scour Kijiji to see if there was any used equipment I might need.

And then it was time! Waves of excitement and total fear washed over me as I drove to my first development class. I convinced myself that this was a good thing—I'm a big fan of the book *Feel the Fear and Do it Anyway*, and I believe you should step outside your comfort zone on a regular basis. But ... was this too far? Were these hockey women going to be scary? Would I be able to keep up? Would I break something? Would someone punch me in the head?

I had been to this community centre arena many times for my son's hockey games, but this felt different. I tried to walk in like a boss with my enormous borrowed-from-my-son hockey equipment bag and stick, but I failed miserably, tripping down the stairs with the bag flipping over and jamming me into a doorway! All the time my son had been doing hockey I realized I had never once helped with this ridiculous bag ... probably because I was always wrangling something a little more crazy—my younger son. We always saw other kids in charge of their own bags and sticks, so we told Zak he needed to do that too. I just never realized how heavy and awkward it was! Just as I was wondering where I should head ... the rink area, which dressing room, hmmmm ... a friendly voice asked, "Are you here for senior women's hockey development?" Thank goodness: "Yes, I am!" I said. With a smile, she directed me to changeroom #1 or 3. As I entered, there were two women behind me who seemed to be there for the first time as well (phew!) I plopped myself down onto the changeroom bench ... I had been getting Zak into his hockey gear since the start, so I'd be okay getting myself dressed, I thought. Deep inhale. I took the first piece I saw out of my big jumble of a bag. It was the chest protector. Easy, I thought. I got this! I remembered to put the neck guard on first and then the chest guard ... awesome, I was feeling like a pro. By now there were a few other women in the room starting to get armoured up around me. The women chatted to each other; no one asked who I was or what I was doing there yet. I kept my head down, trying not to look around too much, trying to appear natural when I was feeling anything BUT natural in this situation. As I started to get all my lower body protection, socks, and skates on, I glanced up at the women around me to see where they were at and realized I had made the rookie mistake in dressing yourself for hockey. I immediately made a note to self: If your mommy isn't there to get you dressed, you'd better start with the lower part first, as it's super difficult and uncomfortable to get your leg stuff on and especially your skates tied with all that bulk up top! I was finally dressed, with ten minutes to spare. By then the changeroom was pretty full, so I decided that instead of sitting around looking and feeling confused, I'd venture out to the arena to wait. Other players were chatting together around the rink while the Zamboni finished up. I stood there awkwardly alone for a while, trying to figure out how to drink from my Gatorade bottle through my helmet cage. Attempting this, I spilled the sticky liquid all over my caged-in face, getting next to nothing in my mouth. As I was trying to wipe my face off through the cage—which I'm sure made me look a bit like I was picking my nose—two friendly women in matching black and yellow jerseys came over and asked me which team I was on. I admitted my newbie-ness to them; they seem seasoned and assured me that all would be fine. The rink gate opened, and the women started filing onto the ice. We were about twenty in line, and I waited until the end to enter, as I knew it would be a very cautious stumble onto the ice for me. The fewer people who beheld my clumsiness, the better, I thought. This backfired, though, as the teacher was right behind me witnessing my struggle! But then I was out on the ice skating with everyone else—whee! I felt okay for a moment, almost secure that my beginner-ness was hidden for now. People were warming up doing laps, a few with pucks. Skating around the rink felt good, fun. I grabbed a puck too and attempted some stick handling. Others were shooting as they passed the nets, but I didn't go that far yet. I just tried to avoid getting in the way as the shooters skated by. I kept envisioning a puck smashing into my teeth whenever I saw anyone slap-shooting or chipping the puck near me, even though I knew I had the full cage on my helmet to protect my face. Soon the teacher called us over to one end of the rink—class was starting! We went through a lot of the same things Zak had learned through the years in hockey ... c-cuts, inner/outer edge turns, crossovers, skating backwards, all in circles and around pylons. Somehow, I was second in line on my side, and I so desperately wanted to tell everyone who seemed to know what they were doing to go ahead of me so I wouldn't slow them down, but instead I determined to step up to this challenge without whimpering. "I can do this," I whispered to myself ... and I did. I was a little shaky, but I got in there and I did it. My sharp turns were not too sharp, my crossovers didn't really cross over, and the teacher had to keep reminding me to bend my knees more, not to bob up and down on my backward c-cuts, and to get comfortable falling. I had heard this last bit of advice so many times—my son's power skating class even had a drill where they repeatedly threw themselves down across the ice and practised getting back up quickly. Fall, get right back up! Literally here, though this is an amazing life skill: don't be so scared of falling down that you don't put yourself out there—when you fall down, pick yourself back up pronto and get on with stuff. And falling with protection is never as bad as you think it's going to be. Almost fun actually! Falling *will* happen if you're trying new, hard things. Our instructor yelled out to us, "If you're not falling, you're not taking enough risks or challenging yourself enough!"

"If you're not falling, you're not taking enough risks or challenging yourself enough!"

Soon pucks were added to the skating drills. It was 10:30 at night, I was exhausted, my head was pounding from the too-tight helmet, my feet hurt from gripping onto my husband's too-big skates, and my lower back, ouch. I've been told that your back hurts if your core isn't strong enough to support the constant squatting position you need to master in hockey. I thought this class was an hour long. As I wondered if it would ever end, the teacher launched into a whole lesson on how to shoot. I hung in there, and we practiced shooting against the boards for what felt like an eternity. Next, we all huddled together. The young teacher wanted to talk plays, madly drawing diagrams alternating between his board and the arena glass, talking a mile a minute ... "defense ... pass ... blue line ... centre ... backcheck" (what did that even mean?) "hashmark ... shoot!" Everyone looked like they were hearing him, understanding, and ready to do whatever this drill was. "Got it? Let's do this!" WHAT??? A rainbow of jerseys glided off to various places on the rink matter-of-factly, ready to "do this!" I thought about standing in the corner alone working on my crossovers; I thought about pretending I needed to go to the washroom, but instead I pushed on and lined up somewhere, asking everyone around me what the heck we were supposed to be doing. A few people tried to explain it to me, I still didn't know, but off I went! Not sure what I was supposed to do ... there I was, doing something with some people and a puck!

Then the trainer announced that we were going to play a fun eight-on-eight game with TWO pucks! I had been worried about being able to follow one puck, and now I had to try to keep track of two? The idea of a game both terrified and excited me. I had never even played a pick-up game of any sort. He split us up into teams—yellow, black, purple, and red jerseys against teal and white jerseys. He dropped the pucks and we were off! I got right in there and actually touched the puck a few times. I was so relieved that others were laughing and squealing like me about their slip-ups and misses. There were no breaks, and it was exhausting. It was also the most fun I had all night! Class ended around 11 pm, and everyone grabbed their water bottles and skated off to the changerooms. I collapsed onto the changeroom bench and looked around the room full of rosy smiling faces, everyone also collapsing around me. And I thought, "This. This is awesome." Really wishing I had a mom or dad to take all this sweaty equipment off me, I somehow mustered the energy to start peeling down. The woman next to me animatedly displayed her crotch, pointing out the sweat pattern made by her gear on her leggings; we giggled—we were all sweaty! I said goodbye to a whole roomful of new friends and walked out into the night skillfully balancing that giant hockey bag and stick in one hand and gulping my Gatorade with the other. Other players with big bags and sticks were the only people in the usually bustling community centre parking lot. It was well past my bedtime, but I was feeling hardcore! Aaaarrrrrrr!

The Sunday of my very first hockey game EVER arrived! I had been waiting for this for what seemed like ages, but as game time drew closer, so many questions and concerns filled my head ... How would

I know when to get off the ice for a shift change? What position would I be playing? What if I stood in the wrong spot at face-off? What if I hurt someone? What if I broke something? Oh, why hadn't I studied my son's games more?

Game day started out like a regular Sunday for me ... early morning hockey practice for Zak, brunch out at our favourite spot, a little catch-up housework throughout the day. When mid-afternoon hit, I realized I'd have to start getting ready for my big game. I changed my clothes, made sure all the many pieces of my hockey gear were packed in my giant hockey bag, and generally worried about how it would all go down. I told my family they weren't allowed to come watch me play until I felt a little more confident that I could actually do it ... and if I'd ever go back. But I guess they were almost as excited as I was (or wanted some comedic entertainment?) and they talked me into letting them drive me to the arena. I remembered this arena, as my son had played a game there the year before. We had been running late and couldn't figure out where it was, so the drive was chaotic. A big argument had ensued, and my husband almost turned the car around and headed home before we got there! This time, we made it there with no issues. As we pulled into the parking lot, I started to lose my courage and tried to tell my people that maybe we shouldn't go in. My husband stopped me and offered, "Let's just go in and have a look around, see how you feel."

I thought to myself about all the seemingly scary things I had done throughout my life ... fitness bikini competitions, belly dancing for thousands, having babies, but this ... this somehow felt scarier than any of that stuff. But stepping out of the car, grabbing my stick and bag—I felt I needed to be brave, if only to send an inspiring message to my kids.

Inside, I was again asked, "Are you here for senior women's hockey?" (Jeez, why did they have to call us seniors? It could just be women's hockey, right?) I couldn't help feeling anything but senior, there with all my boys bringing me to my first game, making sure I got signed in and into the right changeroom. The woman who greeted me was one of the organizers that I had been e-mailing about info and registration, and she was also my team captain. They didn't have a jersey for me for this game, but as luck would have it, the jersey I had scored second-hand at the thrift shop was teal, my team's colour! I'd wear that and my mismatched blue-and-white hockey socks for this first game and was promised a proper jersey for the next week. After my boys wished me lots of luck (I was going to need it), I was off to get ready.

It was just me and the team captain in the changeroom as I started to gear up. I was careful not to make the mistake of putting my upper stuff on before my lower stuff and skates as I did last time. As I pulled on my chest protector, I noticed it smelled a little less than fresh, probably from having been shoved in a bag and left in my car trunk instead of being aired out. It was nothing compared to my son's hockey bag smell, but I was playing with the *ladies* now; I made a note to myself that I'd have to up my gear game as well. Our locker room smelled very different than the ones I was used to being in with my son: I was surrounded by detergent and fabric softener scents—all ocean breeze and cool linen. (Even on the ice you could smell the freshness waft by as players passed you!) Soon more players joined us, and each time someone entered, I was introduced as "Meagan, the new girl!" Everyone seemed super friendly and encouraging. There were lots of questions from everyone: "Where have you played before?" … "Can you skate?" … "I heard you played hockey through university, where?" I hated to disappoint them, but I told them that no, I'd never played hockey or even been to university. "Oh, that's the word on the street, someone just told me that." As the captain was planning the lineup, the big questions came: "Do you shoot left or right?" Suddenly my brain started to race … I was confused and unsure of how to answer that question. Hmmm, I realized I needed to have the stick in my hand to figure it out. Now everyone in the room was looking a little worried as they witnessed my confusion. What hockey player doesn't know which way they shoot? I finally figured it out and told her left … yes left! And then, "What position do you play?" I sensed everyone waiting for my response. "Any?"

My new teammates laughed with me as I told them I'd play whatever position they wanted me to. So, left defense it was ... That was probably best for me, as I thought of myself as more of a defender than a forward scorer. Next came a surprise. Someone announced that we were going to do a pre-game shot of Sour Puss, as it seemed to bring the team luck the week before when they won. Okay, I liked their style already! Little Dixie cups were handed out and filled with bright red Sour Puss. I think the toast was something like, "Fuck You, What the Puck!" (What the Puck was the name of the team we were about to play.) Everyone giggled, cheered, downed the sour alcohol in one swift gulp, and we were off! We filed out into the hall, bumping fists with our five fans, which included my three guys and one other player's family who had come out to cheer us on.

We took our places on the bench while the Zamboni finished cleaning the ice. The husband of one of the players was acting as our coach for the night. I warned him that I had pretty much no clue what I was doing and would need to be pushed around on the ice, yelled at, and whatever else might work. He and the captain both reassured me that it would be fine. I was playing defense on the same shift as the captain, and she took me under her wing and explained where I had to go, exactly when we needed to get out there, how it would all work, how I would know when the shift was over, and how the goalie (who she told me was awesome) would yell at me to tell me who to cover and what she needed from me. Phew! Great! Before I knew it, it was just three minutes until game time and we were skating around to warm up. We did a little cheer-yell-huddle thing, hit our sticks on the ice in unison, and headed back to the bench for the game to start. I tried to take in what the woman playing left defense before me was doing to get an idea for when it was my turn. Which was NOW! Cautiously I stepped onto the ice and booted it over to where I needed to be. The actual game was a blur of fun and stressful action ... so new to me that it was a thrill every time I got to go out and try this thing called hockey. Even sitting on the bench with my fellow teammates was a thrill—all of us sweaty, trying to catch our breath from our previous shift, gulping water, and cheering the players still on the ice. We did approximately one-minute shifts each, and there were just two lineups, so we were working!

On my first shift out I thought I could hear my guys scream, "SKATE!" and "Get up there!" when I was hanging back. Playing defense, I wasn't sure how far up to the other side I should go ... how should I play this? I knew I shouldn't risk leaving our goal exposed, but I didn't want to be of no use to the offense, so I tried to play somewhere around the middle. Oftentimes when I went too far up, the other team's offence would skate down to our side, and as I wasn't a great (or fast) skater, I couldn't catch up and be able to defend. So I started hanging back to be ready for them. I may not have had too many hockey skills yet, but damned if I let that puck get into our net! I did whatever I could. Sometimes that meant skating beside an opponent and throwing them off by kind of poking at the puck that the player was trying to get down the rink. Other times it was one-armed stick flails to reverse the puck away from our side and standing menacingly (I hoped!) in front of the forward that was always waiting near our net. It may not have been pretty, but I was trying hard.

What an amazing feeling the first time I knew I had done something that actually helped my team! I shot the puck away from someone on the other team and way down the ice to their side! I had so rarely had that feeling in life, and it was a rush: "I touched the puck! I touched the puck!" In the end we lost 2 – 3, but we had a super fun time playing!

There were congratulations all around in the changeroom. My teammates told me I had done fine for my first time and asked if I'd be coming back next week. No need to think about that answer: "Of course, and thanks for everything! My first game was awesome!" I hurried to pull my skates and the rest of my gear off, as I could already hear my little one crying for mama just outside in the hallway.

As I rushed out of the changeroom all sweaty and helmet-haired, my baby ran at me, throwing his little arms around my legs in a big hug. My husband said, "Good job!" in an almost believable tone. Zak gave me the talk about how I had been staying back too much and how I really needed to get into the action and be more aggressive. We had had this very same talk with him many times in the past; it meant a lot coming from him, and I'm sure he was happy to be on the other side for once. My husband expressed surprise at how massive I looked in all that hockey gear and offered that I really looked like I was wearing a big old diaper with those shorts.

As we drove home from the arena, my husband helped tweak my strategy, telling me, "You have to keep the puck on their side and don't even think about what if it comes to our side—just keep it way up there!" It made me realize that this was the difference between positive and negative thinking and how sports really could teach life lessons. Here I was, negatively thinking we couldn't possibly keep the puck on the other team's side and I'd better be ready and close to our side for when it comes, when positive thinking would've been more useful: "We will keep it on their side, and if it comes to our side I'll be fast enough to catch it on the way down!" I was determined to go into my next game with this new perspective.

I'm an avid selfie-taker and Instagrammer, so friends who knew I had my first game that Sunday were surprised when they didn't see a pre/post/during game update or photo posting. I had been way too nervous at my first game to even think about snapping a cute selfie in my jersey or anything like that. My husband had mentioned he had taken some photos and video of my very first game, but I hadn't summoned up the courage to have a look that night. A few days later, I finally got up the nerve to ask my husband to show me the videos he had taken. There was a pre-game photo of me looking even more massive than I had imagined, but that was fun, as I knew it was just gear, and everyone looks that way. And there were game videos ... oh the videos made me laugh, and laugh, and then laugh some more! All the problems I knew I had were ultra-magnified. I looked very un-sporty, and at times my backwards skating was more like a weird hop. Then there was my normal forward skating—I looked like I was using the hockey stick as a cane, and instead of bending my knees enough, I was bending my back over the stick. I stayed back from the action on the other side way too much; it made me wonder if my teammates had been annoyed by my uselessness. I nabbed a few screen shots that looked more impressive than the actual video and posted a little collage on Instagram and Facebook, #hockeydreams. Let the likes fly in! Funny thing about social media: from seeing those pics, most of my non-hockey friends would think "Whoa—you're this hockey player now!" But if they had seen the actual game or video footage, they would've seen what an actual mess I was. Watching the videos was hard, but I felt a fresh excitement for the possibilities and learning opportunities ahead of me. I love working towards a really challenging goal, it gets me fired up! Now if only I could figure out how to look cuter in that outfit.. I immediately started thinking of tailoring the jersey just a bit (I had heard some youth rep players actually take their jerseys to tailors!), figuring out those humongous diaper-like shorts, and how best to have my hair tumbling out of my helmet. I realized this wasn't what I was 'supposed' to be thinking about, it was too girly, too superficial. Women should be recognized for more than how they look, yes, but I *wanted* to look great, like an absolute hockey goddess, while tearing up and down that rink, scoring, defending, whatever I needed to be doing!

My second game was a late-night Sunday game. My neighbour who had recommended I join this league told me she hadn't signed up this season because of these late-night games—she just wanted to go to bed at 10 on a Sunday, not start playing a game at that time. After putting my youngest son to sleep, I gathered all my hockey gear (I was—and still am—always paranoid that I will forget some essential item), called goodbye to my husband and son who were downstairs playing X-Box, jumped in my car, and headed to the arena. Scanning through the music in my car, I searched for something to pump me up ... The Gummy Bear Song? No. Elmo Potty Time? No. Jay-Z—that was it! I bumped the volume up to a loud and rare I'm-driving-without-a-baby pitch and rapped along "H to the Izz-o, V to the Izz-A, That's the anthem get'cha damn hands up." I felt like an absolute boss as I pulled into the arena parking. I was running a little late, so I dashed into the building, signed in, and found out what changeroom we were in. I geared up in a hurry, met a few other women on the team that hadn't been there the week before, and then our coach for the night came in to give us a pep talk and outline some strategies and areas to improve on. I tried to take it all in. Then we were off to the ice!

The first period was going great. No one had scored yet, but we had actually kept the puck on the other team's side for most of the period, and it felt good. But about two minutes before the period ended, I was on left defense, there was a flurry of us all crowded around our net, and after a few missed scoring attempts by the other team, one of them chipped the puck off the blade of MY skate and got it in. I felt awful. Guilty. I realized I was just at the wrong place at the wrong time, but my mind immediately shot to "if only I had my stick down at the right place, I could have reversed that puck." Memories of screaming parents at my son's games came flooding back: "STICK ON THE ICE! STICK ON THE ICE!" Where was my loud hockey mom when

I needed her? The player who had scored off my skate looked at me smugly and let out a laugh. As she skated off to high five her teammates, I read the name on her jersey, "Skate Winslet". Humph, cute. I looked back at our goalie and mumbled, "Sorry, that sucked." She just shrugged and gave me a fist bump. I skated back to the bench feeling bummed. The rest of the game went downhill, with the other team scoring more on us with an end score of 3 – 0. I did manage to get in there and shoot the puck out of our zone a lot, so that was exciting, but that first goal that I felt responsible for was still weighing heavy on me. This game seemed more physical with more body slams and people falling. That made it more exciting, as well as terrifying. At one point my fellow defense teammate fell and was down for a bit while we were out there together. I had a moment when I wondered what the protocol was. She was down and not getting up, the game was still going … shouldn't the game pause? Where was the ref's whistle? Should I continue defending the offensive action near our net, or should I see if she was okay? I felt uncomfortable as I continued playing while checking out of the corner of my eye as she lay there on the ice. My natural instinct was to immediately stop playing, help her up and see how she was, but the game just continued. I wondered if maybe these women were tougher than that and she actually might be mad if I let the puck pass us because of this gesture, so I resisted stopping to 'help.' Soon she was back in the game like the big fall had never happened. Once our shift was over and we were both catching our breath on the bench, I asked how she was doing. "It was nothing," came the reply. Really?? That was a big bruiser who had knocked her over, and she had been down for a while, was she sure she was okay? I kept my maybe wimpy thoughts to myself. Then the next thing I knew, the puck was flying over the boards at my face! Luckily, I had a cage on my helmet. I can't imagine wearing no face shield like pro hockey players or even Zak's coaches, who wear no protection on the bench, risking a puck to the face! Why would they do that???

Watching from the sidelines on my off-shifts I reminded myself to think positively: I had to stop thinking defensively. We needed to be aggressive and go at this other team when they had the puck. I tried not to assume the puck was going to end up in our zone ... we could do this. I consider myself a positive person, so it surprised me how I struggled with these thoughts in this context. Every time I rushed out onto the ice for one of my shifts, I tried to force my brain to think this way, but I was still so unsure of my own ability, I found it hard to skate up to someone guiding the puck down the rink with such gusto. I didn't want to just stand there immobile, waiting for her to come to where I was (I had told my son not to do that a hundred times), but going up at them really felt like a risk. I'd overthink.

I'd wonder, "Who am I to challenge this awesome player?" It was a life lesson though: *Take that risk! JUST DO IT!* People always toss around the notion of sports teaching kids so much about life, and here I was, a grown-ass woman learning that they could teach me too. This real-life situation was teaching me more about life, attitude, and positive thinking than I had ever gleaned from any of the self-help books, podcasts, or lectures I had absorbed over my past twenty years as an adult!

The mood back in the changeroom was a little less jolly that night; maybe because we had a big loss, maybe because we didn't have the pre-game shot this time, maybe because it was almost past our bedtimes. Still, it was nothing like when kids lost a game and all kinds of crying, yelling, craziness, and drama ensued. One player showed off her butt shield that was shaped like a big round bum for extra padding (I thought to myself I had enough natural padding there and wouldn't be needing that particular piece of gear!) Others were giving each other pointers and talking about what new wine they had discovered over the weekend. I said my goodbyes, almost picked up the wrong stick from outside the changeroom, #rookiemistake, and left the arena for my car. Feeling a little less boss than when I arrived, I was sweaty, defeated, hungry, and on my way home to a houseful of sleeping guys. But I was proud of myself for doing something so foreign and challenging. I made a note to myself: I needed to get to a stick-and-puck session to practice my skating and speed ASAP!

At the end of a typical busy Saturday, my husband and I were relaxing over dinner, savouring the break and discussing the different hockey happenings of the day. "And when is *your* hockey?" A moment of PANIC! I realized I had totally forgotten I had any hockey this weekend ... What day was it? Had I missed my game? Aaaahhhh—mommy brain! I quickly came to my senses, checked my calendar, and saw that my game wasn't until the next day (Sunday), 8:45 pm. Phew! 8:45 worked better for me than a super early game, which would be right in the midst of bedtime for Jad. I wondered if we could put him to bed a little earlier that Sunday so I could do it all. My husband reassured me that he could handle bedtime on his own and not to worry about it, but I did. That's just me. I like to be able to do my hockey, as long as it doesn't impact anyone else, like the power skating classes I had been taking while the kids were in school, or late-night games once everyone was asleep. I went through moments of feeling awesome and bad-ass for following my heart and playing hockey, but mom-guilt had a habit of creeping in way too often. Sometimes I felt silly for making something I was so bad at (and that wasn't work) a priority. Sometimes I even ended up feeling like I was one of the kids with my hockey classes and games, especially when my husband often denied himself the fun of doing things he wanted to do for fun. He was the one who had passion for hockey from the start. I had tried to get him to play too, but he wouldn't. More guilt: was I hijacking his dream?

The next night I arrived with just ten minutes to spare before game time. I rushed to gear up as I chatted with a fellow teammate, who was tying her skates and taping her shin pads beside me. We were discussing our boys, who had played on the same team a few years ago, which lead to talking about our husbands. For me, it had been an irritating day at home. My husband had been moody, and it had seemed that everyone had a million places they needed to be. That was probably what had caused my husband's moodiness ... he always wanted the kids to do a million activities but would then get annoyed when our whole life was chauffeuring them around and waiting for hours at arenas, dojos, and recreation centres. Anyway, I was happy to get out from under that cloud and go to hockey—something for me! Something to clear my mind and make me smile. The game started; we were playing a familiar team that was about our level, which is always nice. It was still 0 – 0 near the end of the first period. A teammate tagged, "You must be ready to go with that smile!" I replied, "I'm always smiling when I'm playing hockey," and I was off to my left defense position. (I still covertly made an L with my hockey-gloved fingers just to double check that I actually knew where the left side was. I've always been bad at left and right, and I'd hate to confidently skate up to someone else's side not realizing!)

On the bench between shifts that particular night, I had so many thoughts tumbling around in my mind. There's something really special about women's hockey. It's the feminine power. These women, my teammates, the teams we played—they could be fierce and tough as nails at times, bashing into each other, shooting hard, and swearing at the top of their lungs. But they could also switch gears at the drop of a hat and become the opposite: soft, caring, and fun. Laughing with each other, helping each other up, and congratulating one another. At one point I had managed to get the puck away from one of the opposing team's strongest forwards, and she called out, "Nice play!" When a player gets knocked down, it's not uncommon for the player on the other team (who might even have caused the accident) to help her to her feet and check to see if she's okay before continuing to play. You don't see this with boys or men; it's a whole other energy—all aggression and bravado! I tried playing on a co-ed instructional league once made up of mostly men, and the feeling was totally different. I didn't enjoy it.

Until that point, playing hockey had been a kind of scary but overall super fun experience. I was all about trying something new, learning new skills, meeting interesting new people, and I hadn't felt too stupid yet. After a few years, though, playing alongside these amazing, experienced hockey women, I started feeling a bit ... dumb? Irresponsible? Silly? Unsubstantial? Girly? ... I don't know. Maybe it was walking into a changeroom full of hardcore geared-up hockey women in my pink Adidas jacket, matching pink purse, pink-bow Uggs, and long blond hair. Maybe it was when I couldn't for the life of me work the door to the ice at a quick change and someone needed to help me. Maybe it was when I needed to e-mail last minute to tell the team I wouldn't be able to make yet another game for whatever reason. The last straw was the time a ref told me my helmet neck strap was undone and stopped the whole game while he did it up for me on the ice as everyone watched. Like I was a little child. That did it! All of a sudden, I started feeling this inadequacy in all facets of my life and decided I needed to step up to the challenge of being a grown-ass woman in all areas. Over the years in my dance career, I had worked with dancers who made me wonder how they got through life if they couldn't figure out things that seemed easy to me—things like learning choreography, altering a costume, or getting to a show on time. Had I been too harsh on these people? Was I this person in hockey now? Going forward, I vowed to look up where I needed to be for all those face-offs near the net (usually people were pushing me towards where I should be still!), to work on my skating, to stand on the right side of the open door when subbing out. And for goodness' sake, to fasten my own chin strap before stepping onto the ice to play!

Maybe it was my new levelled-up attitude, or maybe it was something else, but my next game renewed my faith in myself. My teammates cheered me on as I took my very first try at scoring with a bit of a slapshot from the blue line. I didn't score, but being up there in the action, trying my hardest, and actually shooting that puck as hard as I possibly could in the right direction felt *good*. And then I tried it again. Still no goal, but I was getting closer, making the goalie sweat a bit—what a rush! I bumped gloves with my teammates as we switched shifts. That evening's game was against a tough team of players who seemed to be younger, stronger, and faster than our team. I was always going up against number 10. Her long platinum hair would blow out behind her helmet as she effortlessly raced past me towards our end. Finally, I had caught up to her before she could try to score. I stood in front of her, trying my best to look tough, a little unsure of what to do other than get in her way and try to poke that puck away from her. She was going to shoot right at me. I wasn't going to let it go into our net (again!). The puck forcefully shot up at me and hit me hard on the one place on my arm that wasn't armoured. "Ouch!" I screamed. There was a quick "Are you okay?" from her, and then we were back at it. I wore my bruised arm like a badge of honour that week; a sign that I had kept the puck out of our net at that moment ... A sign that I had pulled up my big girl hockey socks and was taking charge!

When I was brand new to hockey on my first team, I think they were just excited for me to stumble out onto the ice and maybe touch the puck a few times. As I played more and more, changed teams, and hopefully improved a bit, I finally was at a point where I guess my team thought I was ready to up my game. This team didn't have a husband quasi coach, so during breaks on the bench other players would point things out to me—what I could try, who I should guard, how I should play the player, not the puck. Teammates were passing to me, even when we all knew I might not be the best option, just to give me some experience. This both terrified and excited me! They were screaming at me to catch up to the other team's centre, who was tearing down the ice towards our net trying to score. And it was almost starting to work! During one game, a teammate told me I had to stay on the other side of the blue line if I was going to touch the puck or we'd keep getting offsides. I mentally knew about offsides from watching Zak play and hearing my husband yell "Offside!" every few minutes at every game, but when it came to my own playing and actually staying on the correct side of the blue line as defense, I felt confused all of a sudden. My thinking was that I had to be further back so I could catch up to the other team trying to score; that put me always on the wrong side of the line. I tried to stay on the other side so people wouldn't think I was trying to play forward being all up in the other team's zone. The rest of the game was a bit of a mess as I analyzed all the mistakes I saw I had been making for years. I felt like I had been screwing up my team all this time.

When I got home, I grilled my husband and Zak about everything; about the tips I had been given, about where I should go and when. They were both shocked that I didn't realize what I should've been doing. Zak's advice: "Don't be that defense player who ruins it for everyone," and my husband added, "We always hate defense players who let the puck out of their zone—your whole job up there is to keep it on their side of the blue line." Talking to them helped it all make sense to me, and I felt bad about how I had been playing since I started. Why had no one told me before? But I was also excited to go back the next week and try this new way of playing! The next game I was ready. I felt like a brand-new player on the ice. Yes—I was more in control, more aggressive, and it was awesome! A few people mentioned they saw a big difference in my playing that game. What a great feeling!

Who knows what else I'm still not realizing that I'm doing wrong, but that's the learning curve. I have to believe it'll all happen when I can handle the next level.

Six

Hockey Takes Over

I finally convinced my husband to go to a stick-and-puck session, and I was looking forward to doing this as a fun family outing. I had my own skates now, I'd have to get another helmet for him, and we could share the gear. If anyone in the family should be playing hockey, it was my husband. After all, he was the one who had propelled us all into this world. But his back hurt whenever he'd try, and he was scared that if he fell in a bad way he'd break something. I tried to explain how invincible you felt in all that protective gear, but he wasn't sold. We asked if our across-the-way hockey neighbour's kids wanted to come along to the rink with us, and they did. My husband had the smarts to line up an hour early to sign us all in. We had heard these things often sell out in a matter of minutes and people are turned away once they've sold to capacity. The boys geared up at home, and then we were off to the community centre down the street. In the changeroom, everyone tied on their skates, and I helped my husband into all the gear I usually wore. He admitted he was terrified, but we were off! The arena was packed: hardcore hockey kids and some parents playing pick-up games, doing drills, and working on their stick handling and shooting skills. It was a bit intimidating for novice adults like us. There were little boys, unafraid of anything, weaving recklessly (and with joyful abandon!) around us, smashing pucks at the boards we were hovering around. Luckily Zak had his friends to do hockey stuff with because his parents were hanging at the side of the ice just trying to skate and not fall. My husband confided that his biggest issue was not being able to stop. I tried to share what I had absorbed from a magical three-minute YouTube video that helped me finally grasp how to stop. We worked on our stops for about half an hour. I tried some backward and forward skating techniques I had learnt in classes and practices and hadn't had time to really work on by myself, and then we tried to play a little one-on-one. That was fun, until some rosy-cheeked five-year-old bully stole our puck! At first I thought he had just mistaken our puck for his, but as it continued happening, we realized he was just playing us: he'd steal our puck, then look at us as if to say, "C'mon, let's see you flailing oldsters try to get it back!" Near the end of the session, we suddenly found ourselves playing a bit of a pick-up game with Zak and his friends. I had cautioned my husband not to go there, maintaining we'd stay fine and injury-free as long as we didn't try to play with the kids. But there we were, with the oldest of the three kids on our team taking care of all the shooting and useful things while we both floundered around and tried to distract the other team between almost falling, and then actually falling.

All sweaty and feeling sporty after our hour and a half on the ice, we piled into the crammed locker room and started peeling off our skates and gear, smiles all around. The man next to me exclaimed, "I'm too old for this," then pulled up his pant leg to reveal his un-guarded shin with a huge, bloody hockey stick slash to it! His son assured him that applying some ice at home would take care of it, and I made a mental note to buy another pair of shin guards so my husband and I wouldn't have to share next time. I had gone without guards this time so he could wear mine.

We had heard through the neighbourhood grapevine that years ago there used to be an outdoor rink on the field right behind our house. Looking into this, we discovered that if you got some volunteers together and went through an application process, the city would set up the boards, water supply, hose, and shack so you could make and maintain the rink for community use through the winter. Getting ice time for skating practice and hockey drills is always a big challenge, so my husband jumped at this opportunity. He canvassed a few neighbours, got the required signatures, submitted all the forms to the city, and by November, we were in business!

The boards were up, and we had the combination to the lock on the shack they had built to house the water supply and hose. We studied YouTube how-to videos, devoured anything we could find on the internet about making ice rinks, and talked to a few people about how it had been done in the past. Then we waited for the first big snowfall. First step: pack all the snow down in a flat, even fashion. There are countless YouTube videos showing how to make various machines to roll the snow and level it out. We decided to go with the sled option. Sounds fun, right? It was, for the first fifteen minutes or so. But after a few frantic hours taking turns pulling grown adults around a massive field in a (broken-down, by this point) sled to pack that snow down was a tiring chore. And of course, it was getting later, darker, and colder. By just before midnight, we had kind of levelled and packed down our base—not perfectly—but enough to start flooding the area with water. This, we thought, would be the exciting part, the satisfying part. Turns out it takes a long time just standing there holding that running hose before you even start to see water pooling unless you're using a huge tarp liner. We had originally wanted to use a tarp but couldn't source one large enough at what we considered a reasonable cost. I remember telling my husband I had to go back home after about thirty minutes of hosing. We were both freezing! He was determined, though, and stayed out all alone well into the night filling that boarded-up rectangle in the field behind our home. My son and I watched him in disbelief from a bedroom window which looked out on the park. "Daddy's crazy!" We weren't the only ones who found his determination odd; on subsequent nights he was heckled by various passersby calling out, "Weirdo!" or "What the hell are you doing?" as they saw this lone figure spraying a firehose over a field at midnight in the freezing cold. As the routine continued through the winter, he found a buddy to help him out with some of the cold floods and learned that those little heat packs for your boots and mitts were magical for staying warm.

That winter ended up being a lot warmer than usual, and I was surprised at my uncharacteristic disappointment in the milder weather. I wanted beautiful ice, so I found myself wishing for the coldest weather possible! What? I usually hate harsh, snowy Canadian winters. I'm not one of those people who like winter things ... making snow angels, skiing, skating, walking outdoors—but this winter I was hoping for frost and ice-making weather so we could get this rink up and running. I fantasized about getting up early to start my day with a refreshing morning skate ... all the kids skating and playing hockey over the holidays ... even going for night skates with my son after putting the baby to sleep. The possibilities seemed endless with the rink right in our backyard. I actually felt depressed when I saw above-zero weather forecasts!

My dream of skating with our neighbours did become a reality during a super-cold week or two. One day, looking out our back window, we saw a boy bring his hockey net from home and practice shooting for hours. That was awesome, but was it worth all the crazy late nights my husband had spent out there flooding that rink? Even though we loved the dream of creating a community rink, we vowed to try a smaller, more manageable backyard rink the next year.

After a few years of hockey, our usually lovely office/guest room had turned into a stinky hockey locker room! This was where my son and I would store our massive hockey bags left open so the gear could air out and dry before the next time we used it. I'd try to keep the door to the room shut so the baby wouldn't go in, get busy pulling everything out of our bags, and scatter pieces all over the house (or so the cat didn't pee in the bags, which had happened in the past—yuck). A familiar sweaty arena odour would greet you as you opened the door, and I'm not sure what we'd do if we actually had a guest stay over. But not being a fan of having the bags strewn across our kitchen or living room floors, this was our reality.

We really didn't have many overnight guests, but we did have a lot of hockey going on in our lives. I started planning for this guest room to turn into an actual full-on hockey room with all our spare gear, room to dry out our equipment, storage for all our old jerseys, and decorated with hockey trophies, medals, and photos. One day I casually shared my plan with my mom, and her response shocked me: "But what will happen when you're not into hockey anymore?" With that I began to realize how deeply in it I was when I dismissed that as a super-silly question. And the clues continued. At one time, our neighbourhood was experiencing a lot of car thefts. Cars would disappear from driveways overnight. Waking up one morning and not seeing my car in the driveway, my husband yelled up to me, "I think your car's been stolen!" The first thing that popped into my mind? Yikes, Zak's hockey bag and mine were both in there ... AND OUR STICKS! Never mind the car! It ended up that I had parked in the garage that night, but where my mind went certainly pointed to my hockey-head priorities.

Seven

Hockey Is For Everyone

We had always known there was racism in hockey. My husband and I had met up years before with a man from the University of Calgary who was writing a paper on the topic. He was looking into hockey's role in Canadian multiculturalism, hockey's value in making newcomers feel more comfortable and Canadian, and figuring out what the barriers for entry were and how to fix them. He asked if we'd agree to be part of his research and interviewed our family in a nearby Tim Horton's. Questions covered what we had experienced, how hockey made my husband feel, racism in youth hockey, and what barriers we had encountered.

I'm not even sure how to approach this whole subject. I'm uncertain about what it's okay for me to weigh in on. Because, as a white person, maybe I'm not supposed to understand the impact or grasp the seriousness of racial biases in hockey — especially as it affects youth hockey, where our kids learn about their world. But I don't want to tiptoe around the issue; I want to talk as candidly as I can about what I've experienced. Maybe it'll open some eyes and allow more hockey people to look closely at certain circumstances that play out in our arena life. Maybe people who've never considered these things because they haven't had to, because they're not attached to someone affected by these biases like I am (my husband is Arabic, and both our young players have a distinctly non-WASP appearance). Change is needed, but awareness must always come before change.

Whenever we've looked at prospective teams, we've always tried to search out a team that has a coach who isn't white. Or if he was white, we'd try to suss him out. How easily did a racist comment slip off his tongue? Just how 'exclusive' does he try to keep his team? I don't like to think this way, and I don't like my kids to see this, but it's part of our reality as a blended Arabic-Canadian family within today's sport of hockey with oftentimes frankly racist overtones. That may sound harsh, but it's the reality we live with. Most rep-level coaches are older white men—they're there because they have the experience and love the sport—and I'm not saying all older white men are automatically racist, but we have met many in the hockey world who are. The few POC coaches usually boast more of a diverse team comprised of various cultures and colours, which makes us feel more welcome. With a team like this, we wouldn't have to endure the standard racist questions and joking around. Most old man white coaches have teams full of blond, blue-eyed players. One coach my husband spoke to actually admitted to weeding out would-be players for his team by only inviting kids with French and Russian last names: "Those are the real hockey types, it's in their blood!" These teams sometimes have a few token ethnicities—usually one stand-out black player that everyone marvels at for his height, maybe one Asian that people commend for his hard work, with perhaps a few 'questionables' like us — "What mix do you think that kid is? What was his last name?" And that's about it. When you're on a team like this, you naturally bond with the few others that are on the same page. They're usually the first to come up and introduce themselves, after you've both locked eyes when too many people around you start openly discussing your son's tan skin colour or their son's afro/helmet mix. I've heard it all; "*Those* people aren't interested in playing hockey, they play basketball, or soccer ..." Maybe they do, but why is that? Are *those* people not playing hockey because they don't like it, or were they pushed out of serious hockey by all the racist claptrap they've encountered? I sometimes wonder why any of 'us' want to be a part of a sport that doesn't really encourage every player to excel and go past rec level.

One year we were invited to some skates with a team in our town. The coach and my husband had bonded a bit over discussing racism within hockey, which doesn't get discussed openly much at all. I guess this man assumed he and my husband shared the same heritage, and he boasted about all the different places from his particular country that the current team's players were from. During a skate one day he told my husband he realized there was no way his children would ever make a rep team because of all the racism. He said he had decided to make his own multicultural team that year and planned to buy a franchise in the future! We had actually dreamt up that exact idea out of desperation a couple of years earlier when we saw how POC were treated in hockey. The coach related tales of the racist graffiti that had been scrawled on the changeroom walls before his team went in and how white people don't believe there's any racism in hockey because they just don't see it. When you're in a family like mine you do see it. I've heard other coaches in the association refer to this man, not by his name, but as 'that coach with the turban'. Or they point him out as a poster child of the 'demographic' change in our town: maybe his presence will help attract more of this different demographic into hockey so it doesn't die. They need him. But don't seem to fully accept him? It's confusing.

We once courted a coach in hopes of getting Zak a place on his prestigious team. For months my husband refused to go to the skates, arguing that it would be best if Zak was accompanied by a parent who looked less 'foreign.' I was totally against the plan because I don't like to think that way. My husband maintains that that's just me not seeing racism because I'm white and people aren't racist towards me. Then I wonder, if it's all true, why would we ever want to be on that team? But what my husband says makes sense in one way: eliminating all the teams that might be thinking along those lines means we'd have maybe three teams to try out for instead of thirty. And competition is stiff, even with thirty prospective teams. So, I went along with my husband's strategy and took Zak to all the skates and try-outs. One night the coach finally asked the burning question as we discussed Zak's fit on the team: "So, what origin is your last name?" I guess my Arabic surname doesn't fit my look. I sputtered out, "Hesham is Arabic. My husband is Arabic," knowing very well that my husband would not like that I had divulged this. Not after carefully concealing this the whole time so we would appear like a 'normal' white hockey family. My husband had (half-) joked many times about using my maiden name instead of his surname for our kids' hockey careers to avoid discrimination and questions like this. Had I just blown it? After making some comment about, "Oh, that's where Zak gets his tan complexion from, eh?"

the coach continued on to let me know that my son would not be on the team that year, but he tossed out, "We'll keep in touch." No surprise: we/he did not keep in touch.

You know that feeling when you're standing around near a group of people, you're looking at them, catching a few lines of their conversation back and forth although not purposely eavesdropping; you're just all there together? And you can't help automatically forming some thoughts about what you're seeing and hearing, making some generalizations about them? Well, that's what I was doing one Friday night in the arena lobby while I was waiting for Zak's practice to start. Five burly, middle-aged white men encircled the star trainer that had just been instructing their children. I overheard, "There was a little oriental man who wanted to speak to you ..." My chest tightened, I felt sick. I stepped away. I could tell where this was going ...

I know that jumping to generalizations, painting everyone with the same brush, is wrong. It's like people automatically thinking a group of veiled Muslim women are part of a terrorist group. But sadly, I'm usually right about these groups of hockey dads, and I've gotten to see more of them in the last few years. Overhearing this group of hockey dads discussing the little 'oriental' man that was looking for the trainer made me angry even before anything more was said. It was easy for me to imagine the barrage of racist comments that would fly easily off their tongues with a laugh at any minute. I had heard it so many times before. Before more was said, I was already embarrassed for them, for me, and for the man looking for the coach. I thought to myself, would they say there was a little white man looking for the coach? Or better yet, a big-ole cracker looking for the trainer? If he hadn't been another ethnicity than white, there would have been no reference to his appearance, background, heritage, or ethnicity. I tried to breathe and calm myself. I tried to convince myself that maybe the rest of this conversation would go another way. Maybe they'd surprise me. I made small talk with my husband, still half-listening to the men. There seemed to be some joking about this man looking for the trainer, who then approached the group and wanted to talk to the trainer in front of all these hockey dads. I couldn't watch. As we walked away, I mentioned it to my husband. He admitted he had also been eavesdropping and expecting the worst. He never would've brought it up if I hadn't ... I guess because he's so used to that sort of behaviour by now. My husband tells me, "You only notice it because you're with me." I want to believe, though, that I would notice and be affected by it even if we weren't together. I would. I know I would.

Later that night, I saw a man exiting the rink wearing a hoodie that read in big, bold caps 'CHANGE HOCKEY CULTURE!' Staring at the words across his chest, so many emotions were running through me ... gratitude, disbelief, curiosity, and ... hope? I was in mid-conversation with another mom about the possibility of taking her son with us to an upcoming practice, as she'd be working a long shift, so I didn't get a chance to ask the man about the words on his shirt. As I chatted with the hockey mom, in true nerd fashion, I typed 'CHANGE HOCKEY CULTURE' into the notes on my phone so I could look up what that was all about later. The minute I got home I excitedly typed the words into Google. Google took me to www.hockeydiversityalliance.org—the group who got together with hockey company Bardown to make this hoodie. Sadly, the merch was all sold out, so I couldn't order a shirt, but I got to learn about the Hockey Diversity Alliance (HDA), whose mission is "to eradicate systemic racism and intolerance in hockey." Powerful and to-the-point. I had to keep reading about this amazing Calgary-based initiative. I found out that the HDA was started by Akim Aliu and other NHL greats like Trevor Daley, Evander Kane, Nazem Kadri, Wayne Simmonds, Matt Dumba, Anthony Duclair, Chris Stewart, and Joel Ward. They had teamed up with Budweiser, Heinz/Kraft, and Scotiabank to deliver their message.

Seeing this website with the ads and slogans on clothing validated in some way that it wasn't all just in our heads; that my husband and I hadn't blown things out of proportion. Before this, I had often felt that people didn't really talk about the culture of racism in hockey. It was just sort of swept under the rug. Nobody spoke up about it because ... you wanted to fit in, you wanted your kid to play hockey and not stick out, you wanted to feel Canadian. Even when you met and connected with another person you suspected was going through the same race-related issues in the hockey world, there would be some sort of tacit agreement to keep silent. To mention nothing. Nobody ever really talked about being the only Singh, Wang, or Hesham amongst a whole lot of Smiths, Bakers, and Thompsons. Nobody talked about how the majority of all the rep hockey coaches are old white men. Coaches and hockey dads had been out drinking with my husband, sharing and laughing at racist jokes and stories. He's come home from a night out with 'the boys' wondering, "Who exactly do they think I am?"

The biases, the racial stereotyping, the discrimination was something we didn't want to believe, but it was right there all around us. And we found it was worse the further into hockey we ventured; the higher up we went. To be fair, we've met the best of people in hockey as well. We've had a few amazing coaches who were very accepting and inspiring—mainly younger men who perhaps hadn't grown up in as homogeneous a world as their older counterparts. Seeing that man in his 'Diversity in Hockey' hoodie opened my eyes to the fact that there were actually people out there trying to bring awareness to the issue that had weighed heavily on my heart for so many years. Then I started noticing things popping up everywhere shedding light on hockey's racism problem. Scotiabank started a campaign with posters and a commercial that featured racist remarks like "Shouldn't he be playing basketball?", "Do they even have ice in China?", or "Shouldn't this guy be coaching cricket?" Disparaging comments directed at women in hockey and bullying directed at sledge hockey and LGBTQ players all jumped to life on the screen. At the end of the ad, a Black player is taunted with the phrase, "Go back to where you belong!" P.K. Subban responds, "Go back to where we belong? This is where we belong." And the tagline appears: 'Hockey for All.' It's so moving I almost tear up, but instead I feel my face flush with a mix of anger … and excitement. It's a start.

Budweiser teamed up with the HDA for the Tape Out Hate campaign, which featured a two-minute video of a real, very candid roundtable discussion in a locker room with NHL stars of colour. Akim Aliu says he was ten years old when an opposing team member's parent used a racial slur against him for the first time. Wayne Simmonds had a banana thrown at him during a game. Almost immediately the question was asked: "Why would you ever want your child to experience something like that? Would you put them in hockey?" And the response? "If I knew she was going to have to face what I faced, probably not."

Part of the campaign was hockey tape that read 'TAPE OUT HATE!' and 'RACISM HAS NO PLACE IN HOCKEY!' I wished with all my heart that we didn't need these messages or tape that basically say, "Hey, hockey's for everyone—don't be an ass!" But I knew we needed it, all of it. Finally, there's the start of some awareness. Change is needed.

Eight

Pandemic Setbacks and Silver Linings

When the Covid-19 pandemic hit, one of the biggest changes to our lives wasn't switching from in-person to online school or missing out on enjoying meals at restaurants, it was no more hockey. No more hockey friends, no more hockey sweat, no more hockey talk. With everything shut down, our current hockey season was cut short with no finals, and our whole try-out/look-see skates for rep teams was rudely interrupted. After a couple months of hockey lockdown, we started to worry. Not only about our son losing skills he'd been working on, like his edgework and his shots, but also about how unhealthy it was for him to be sitting around playing endless video games, staring at his phone, and scarfing down Cheetos. Who knew how long it would be until intense workouts at the arena for hours several times a week would resume?

For a while I had been dreaming of the possibility of synthetic ice tiles for our garage to make a mini home arena/training centre for us. I had researched, checked out all the companies that made them, and calculated how ridiculously expensive it would be to get enough tiles to cover our whole double garage. I considered buying fewer tiles and just creating a shooting pad, but I knew we'd really want to be able to practice skating stuff as well as shooting. When it seemed like there was no end to the lockdown in sight and that we might *never* be back in the arena, an investment in synthetic ice finally made sense. We committed and ordered five boxes of HockeyShots synthetic ice tiles to make our dream of a home practice arena come true! The tiles arrived about a week later, and we got to work clearing out the garage and clicking those tiles together. It was a family effort, and we felt excited to have all the tiles in place. After treating the surface with slide spray, we all laced up our skates, ready to try it out. My husband and I loved it. Zak wasn't such an instant fan: "It's fine, it's just not like real ice, it's a whole other way of skating, it won't transfer." It *was* different, but we knew this was somewhere he could at least practice his shooting. I think I used it more than he did, working daily on my crossovers, shooting, and more. And having a rink in our garage did get us all out there playing some fun two-on-two shinny, usually me and Jad against my husband and Zak.

Four months into the pandemic, we got word that hockey might start up again soon in some way or another. Talk was around smaller groups, no dressing rooms, no parents allowed in, no face-offs, no contact, perhaps full plastic face shields instead of wire cages on helmets, maybe even face masks under the helmet cage? Whatever the rules, we were in! A few of our old hockey friends were putting together a small team for a four-on-four league happening in the town next to us at a private facility that was supposed to start as soon as we entered the next phase of 'reopening,' and we wasted no time signing up. But as the date grew closer, that got postponed, as the province hadn't qualified for Phase 3 of reopening yet.

In the meantime, we learned that one of Zak's trainers was going back to teaching small groups at private facilities. He'd e-mail all the interested parents a few days before a session, and whoever wrote him back quickest would get a spot. This guy had a very committed following—he was a straight-shooter and told kids and parents what they needed to hear even though sometimes it could be harsh. He was tough. At Zak's first class, the trainer assigned him to stay in a total squat the whole class (including when they were waiting), told him he had been stick-handling wrong this whole time, and that his skating needed to be more on his toes. We appreciated that he told us more within that first hour of meeting us than any hockey coach or teacher had told us throughout all our years of hockey. We immediately wanted more; Zak had different feelings and thought the coach was a bit mean. We responded to his e-mails as soon as we saw them but kept being told we hadn't been quick enough to make it into the group of nine he could teach. (Probably a bit of a relief to our son.) The third week of our lightening-quick attempts, we were in!

We hadn't been inside an arena in what seemed like forever and looked forward to the class date. The session was taking place at an arena in a neighboring town. Gathering together Zak's hockey stuff, we realized we had forgotten to sharpen his skates after all that synthetic ice-tile skating. Of course, no one at any Canadian Tire could do it that morning on our way to the arena! Zak's sudden growth spurt over the break from hockey meant his skates were suddenly too small, and my skates that he'd been wearing poked him in a weird way when he wore them for more than ten minutes. He had even sort-of forgotten how to get himself dressed, putting on his hockey sock without a shin guard. We had been told he'd need to get dressed in the arena parking lot and walk in fully dressed with his skates on. Uh oh, that meant he'd need skate guards. I figured we must have a pair of skate guards *somewhere*. I hunted around frantically and could only turn up one, so we tied a towel around his other skate, and off he hobbled into the arena all alone for the first time! No parent spectators were allowed in, so he was on his own without anyone in the stands shouting the usual encouragements to "Skate hard!" and "Stick on the ice!"

Determined to be more prepared for our next rink time, we spent the week getting organized. We bought Zak new skates—fancy skates—at a special hockey store, not just randoms off the Canadian Tire clearance shelf. We even got them molded to his foot and profiled; all the real fancy hockey stuff we had heard about from other parents through the years but had never actually done ourselves so far. We remembered to get new skate guards that he could wear in and out of the arena. We showed up early to the far-away arena for our second session with the star hockey coach.

There were lots of hockey families hanging out in the parking lot around pickup trucks and SUVs, kids getting dressed out of the back of vehicles, as changerooms weren't allowed at that point. After filling out the waivers and dropping Zak off at the door so the teacher could escort him inside to the rink, we hung out in the scorching Saturday morning sun in the opened-up back of our SUV. Looking out at the sea of hockey parents waiting around in the parking lot just like us, it dawned on me once again: hockey parents are a whole other breed. They, well, I guess WE, are more than a little bit crazy! At times it seems almost cult-like, the following that youth hockey has, with parents discussing all the options, obsessing about teams, coaches, fancy equipment, and training ... and hanging out in parking lots in the middle of a pandemic, waiting hours for their junior hockey stars to finish their expensive, special hockey session!

I had always known I was kind of over-the-top and super dedicated as a hockey mom, but the pandemic really highlighted how powerful hockey had become in my life. With hockey slowly opening up again, new opportunities popped up all over. Of course we wanted to do it all, just throw ourselves back into the beautiful world of hockey. Four months into the coronavirus situation, Zak was starting a four-on-four league with some old hockey friends. He probably wasn't as stoked about it as his over-zealous hockey parents were. We were advised that the organization would be taking a lot of precautions to reduce risks: no changerooms/come ready or change in parking lot, no face-offs or body contact during play, face masks worn until kids are on the ice, and only one parent allowed into the arena to watch. We had always been that weird family who did everything together; not just games, but 7 am practices, late-night/far-away power skating sessions, weekend out-of-town tournaments, try-outs. We'd all schlep to everything. I loved it, and we looked at hockey as fun family time together. Until then, no parent had been permitted in with kids for the classes we were doing; now, only *one* parent was allowed to watch the game. How could they do this to us? It was 'decided' (for some reason) that my husband was the lucky one that would go, and I would stay at home with our youngest. All the hockey moms were chatting about finally seeing each other again and who would be at the game in our WhatsApp hockey mom group. I envied the moms whose husbands would be coaching, as they both could go (one coaching, the other as a spectator), as well as the single moms, as there'd be no question about who would go. I even envied the reluctant hockey moms who were relieved not to have to go to a game. When my husband and Zak left for the game, I felt totally left out of the fun. That's when it hit me how much hockey really meant to me personally and to us as a family. I realized how great it was that I had started to play hockey myself ... thinking about what happens to crazy hockey parents when their children choose to stop hockey, or grow up and don't make it to the NHL. Support group needed! Is there a support group? There's a kind of eccentric (maybe a little drunken) old man who hangs out at hockey arenas around the area, watching random kids' hockey practices and games. Though this may sound a bit creepy, he's explained to us many times over a cup of snack bar coffee that he used to pretty much live at arenas with his two sons when they played rep hockey. Now they're grown men, and he missed it. I can relate. That could happen to me! So, playing hockey myself and putting my energy towards that is like insurance against that possibility. At the same time, it takes the stress off my children to be the sole hockey entertainment for the family. The night's game gives my husband and I lots to talk about afterwards: what happened, how Zak did, the stresses of playing hockey in the middle of the pandemic, and of course catching up on news and gossip of all the other parents we haven't seen for ages!

After several weeks of not being able to go watch the four-on-four games, the team's coaches (fellow hockey parent friends) planned a camping trip. Our family had opted out. I may have been feeling more Canadian through hockey, but not so Canadian that I thought camping sounded like fun! As we'd be at home while the coaches were pitching tents in the woods somewhere, my husband and I were approached about taking over as substitute coaches for the game on Saturday. I was super excited. I immediately ordered a typical hockey coach outfit from Amazon for my debut as a coach! I am so far from a believable boys' hockey coach, but I was serious about at least *looking* the part, and I felt that the windbreaker warm-up pants-and-jacket set would help me pull it off. The outfit was a throwback, reminding me of what I used to wear in my late teens working at gyms. Oh, I realized that I wasn't going to be actually 'coaching'. My biggest duty would probably be opening and shutting a door for the players to quickly come and go for their shifts, but I was still excited. Would we know what we were doing? My husband had helped coaches out a few times when the assistant coach hadn't been there, so he kind of knew what to expect, but I had never had an opportunity like that. It's rare to see a female coach or a mom helping out on the bench. I think I've seen *one* ever in all my years of watching kids' hockey. When I saw that one female coach, I was super impressed and inspired—it could happen. And now, here was my chance! Gathering extra jerseys for our sub players and hockey tape out of the car trunk at the arena, I started thinking that all these hockey dads might wonder why *they* weren't helping coach with my husband instead of me. One dad used to co-coach a three-on-three team with my husband a few summers back. What if that was what he was talking to my husband about, just steps away in the parking lot? Why *had* they asked me? Doubt and insecurity washed over me as I thought about passing my job over to him. But I had bought those coach windbreaker pants ... So, I looked down and pretended to focus on tying my son's skates. Then I pulled on a very coach-y looking cap, screwed up my bravado, and walked confidently over to say hi. As we met up with the parents and the rest of the team, I started thinking that a few of these hockey dads would be more qualified for my job. Managing to push that thought aside, I signed in and led the kids into the arena. As the players waited to go on the ice, I madly scribbled down the names of a bunch of kids I didn't know yet on a game paper I needed to immediately hand back to the ref. I whispered to my husband, "Do you know what we're doing?" He let out a nervous laugh and said, "Not really."

Off we went! My husband had the defense lined up where the forwards should be. Uh oh, at least I knew that much from playing myself, so we switched that around. My husband was stationed at the forward door, and my job was defense. Suddenly, the game began. I was in charge of making sure there were enough changeovers, yelling at the two skaters on the ice or rattling the door when they should come back and switch. It went smoothly—those eleven and twelve-year-olds were more mature than I thought they'd be—they knew what they were doing. Sometimes the women I play with need to be reeled in for their break and told to let another player take over. But these guys always came back willingly after about a minute and a half of playing to take a break and let some fresh players get out on the ice. The team was a mix of levels ... A, AA, and even one AAA player, and they were very good. The big AA boys were yelling things at my son like "Shoot!" and "Hurry up!" not knowing (or caring) that I was his mom. I felt a little bad but tried to stay focused on when to open the door for these defensemen. Only once did I get so caught up in the game that one of them had to yell "DOOR!" at me. It's funny because senior women hockey players do this—we don't have the luxury of doormen. I understand now why it's important to have three coaches: two assistant coaches/doormen and then the head coach in the middle who can focus on actually coaching the players. I was so focused on my job that I didn't even realize we were winning or who scored what. And my hands were freezing! Finally, the game was over, a 3 – 4 win for us, and we hurried out of the frigid arena into the warm summer day. Later my husband told me that the dad he was talking to *had* asked who was coaching with him and volunteered that he could coach with him anytime he needed someone. Was he implying that my husband was so desperate he *had* to use me? I didn't dwell on that, realizing that hardly anyone knew how into hockey I was myself. I watch it, I play it, I read about it, and that day ... I had been part of the coaching team! That happy thought stayed with me as we talked hockey on our drive home.

We've always struggled with finding the right balance of encouraging Zak to get better, practice, do more, etc. as we would as motivated adults, while letting him guide us about what he wants to focus on and do. Were we pushing too much? Not enough? It was difficult to know. Zak once trained with a private hockey teacher who cautioned us that *his* parents had pushed and pushed so hard that it eventually caused him to hate the game; he left playing when he was old enough to make that decision and had only come back recently to coach and share his message with overbearing hockey parents. I tried to reason with my husband, suggesting that I didn't think many twelve-year-old boys are naturally begging to be signed up for strict hockey training camps or jumping out of bed for the chance to shoot the puck in the garage a hundred times before breakfast. I think most twelve-year-olds are like Zak—a little lazy, way too into video games, gaming with friends, and content to sit staring at a screen for hours on end (or until we pull him away from it). I'm convinced it's parents' influence, expectations, and scheduling that is the determining factor at that age. My husband has a habit of asking Zak if he *wants* to do this hockey camp, or class, and expecting the answer *he* hopes for will be forthcoming. When he gets a less-than-enthusiastic response or a sarcastic answer, he gets so mad. I think we should decide what he's doing at this age and just tell him. Presenting a kid with too many options, having so many wrong/upsetting choices (to the parent) is a problem. It's like asking a kid, "Do you want to tidy up your room now?" when "NO THANKS!" or "Maybe tomorrow" are not 'acceptable' answers. When I see what some moms write in various hockey mom Facebook groups I'm part of, how their sons are - *dying* to get back on the ice after Covid or are practicing their edgework into the wee hours on their backyard rink, I wonder. Is that what the moms want to think? The picture they need to present? I'm not saying that there aren't some kids who may have a dream very early, coupled with a fairly grown up one-mindedness that motivates them to do whatever it takes to make that dream a reality, but I think they may be in the minority. Maybe some kids really are like that. Maybe my question is: if mine doesn't display that level of engagement or motivation without parental intervention, does it mean he's just not that into it?

Looking back, I tried to remember at what age I started getting obsessed with dance. How old was I when I began taking the initiative to practice and better myself without a parental prompt? I can't remember my mom ever telling me to practice, but then, I wasn't a very skilled dancer until late into my teens after I had taken it upon myself to become a better, more professional dancer. Sure, everyone likes the idea of being in high-level hockey. Sure, my son wants to go around saying, "I play triple A," but the work it takes to make that happen is less appealing. I often think my son and husband should just *tell* everyone he's on whatever impressive double A, one year up, amazing hockey team they desire, and then Zak should go be happy playing some house league! Because sometimes that seems to match what my son really would like.

U13 and U14, or Pee Wee and Bantam, is the age class where a lot of kids start dropping out of hockey. We had noticed a definite shortage of players as they got older. There are many possible causes; it could be high school, social life, hormones, dating and romance, kids simply coming into their own and discovering new interests. How *do* you know when your child wants out of the hockey world? Around this age, mine had developed a sudden and all-consuming obsession with Kung Fu. Instantly I saw the motivation that we had always found missing in hockey. Zak would practice kicks in the kitchen while waiting for breakfast, read all the Kung Fu books he could get his hands on, watch endless videos on the coolest forms and punches, and be super bummed if he had to miss a Kung Fu class, especially if it was because it clashed with a hockey game time. I started wondering if hockey was done for Zak. Or was Kung Fu just a shiny new thing for him as hockey had been at one point? Were we the ones holding on to the hockey dream? Or did he want it too? Asking him, trying to involve Zak in this discussion, was always met with a somewhat indifferent response. Sometimes it would lean a little more towards the hopeful or positive side, but I questioned how much of that was just to please his parents ...

For some reason, Canadians seem so surprised and caught off-guard when we have our first big snowfall of the season. We're never ready with the snowplows and salt, everyone's stuck in the snow, there's lots of crazy driving—no one ever seems to expect it, even though it happens every year around the same time. Each November or December everyone acts like they haven't seen snow like this in twenty years! I never understand it. So, there we were, quite literally freezing our buns off sitting on the cold hard benches at one of the most notoriously frigid arenas in town. It was our team's home rink, so we were all there a lot, and as often happens, the big heater above the spectator benches wasn't on. In all the years at this arena for practices, games, try-outs, and classes, I've never once seen it heating the few rows of benches it looms over. But as usual, parents were complaining loudly, "The heat's not on!" and shaking their heads before heading to the lobby for some warm-up time. Practice hadn't started yet, but some keeners were on the ice warming up already. As we saw Zak moseying out of the changeroom—last as usual—I sprinted over to pass him his water bottle that he had forgotten in the car. Before I went, my husband whispered, "Tell him to have some energy out there tonight; he won't listen to me." I did, and this got me a quick eyeroll from my eldest, which didn't bother me half as much as it would have bothered my husband. Sitting in the rink under that big heater that never comes on, we watched the boys do impressive drill after impressive drill, and I tried to explain to my husband how pulling his face off the Plexiglass, sitting back, and acting a little cool might help. I hit his hands down as he went to give Zak an enthusiastic thumbs-up when he skated by. "Stop! Look away, and act like you don't really care how this goes ... act like this is *his* thing, not yours!" It's like Zak wants to irritate him by doing the total opposite of what he wants. This is the age for that isn't it? If my husband says go right, Zak will fight to go left. If my husband says show some energy out there, Zak will make sure to be super laid back, slow, cool—whatever you want to call it. I pointed out to my husband that Zak's at the age where he needs to feel like it's his idea to really get excited about something. "Why do you think he's so pumped about his new love of Kung Fu and all things Bruce Lee? Because it's his idea, we don't actively encourage it, put him in all sorts of special classes for it, bother him about it" (like we do with hockey). I'm not sure how much of this reasoning got through to my husband.

When Zak first started hockey, we had to go through an online *Respect in Sport Training For Parents* with our hockey association. This ninety-minute-long course dealt with misplaced enthusiasm, balance, and basically taught us that we shouldn't belittle our children about hockey and what they do on the ice. It stressed never holding over their head all the time and money we'd spent on their hockey. When I first did this training, the examples seemed ridiculous ... that didn't really happen, did it? We would never say things like that!

But with each passing year, as we began taking hockey more and more seriously, it all made sense. I'm not proud to say this, but some of the examples used in the course and questions at the end—things I had found too outrageous to be true—came close to what sometimes happened in our household, on drives to games, and after games. There is a necessity for arenas to display big signs everywhere that state:

These are kids.

This is a game.

Parents should cheer for everyone.

Referees are human.

You and your child do not play for the NHL.

These are all part of the 'Relax, it's just a game' campaign. According to the Respect in Sport Course, 70% of kids quit sports by age thirteen because they stop having fun. And the most common reason is parental behavior ... and pressure. Sad, but of course, I wouldn't want to play hockey either if it wasn't fun.

> ## "I wouldn't want to play hockey either if it wasn't fun."

And then it was that time of year again. What would we be doing next season? Would we be invited back on the team we had been playing on? Should we go back down to Zak's actual age team? Should we be talking to other coaches? What was everyone else doing ... A? AA? Coaches started calling ... hinting ... scouts were coming out to watch people at games. Hoping to stop all our wondering, we asked Zak what he wanted to do. We knew how notoriously avoidant he was at making decisions, and we realized he could be especially hesitant about spitting out that he might not want to spend so much time on the family's beloved sport of hockey next year, his first year of high school. He approached it by saying there were so many different options, and he wanted more time to do other things. My husband looked defeated and asked, "Maybe you want to take a break from hockey?" (Of course praying he didn't.) Zak asked how long a 'break' would be, and I told him it would have to be a whole season, and then who knew if he'd ever get to go back. I suggested that he might want to just drop down a level and play recreationally, which would mean just one practice and one game a week—just half of what he had been doing for the past few years. I got a maybe for that. But he still didn't know what he wanted. We would have to know soon! I knew my husband took this all very hard, as he felt his hockey-dad dreams of Zak becoming an NHL superstar were falling apart as we spoke. It had been coming for a while, but this conversation made that possibility hit home. Later that night, I tried to explain to my husband that there *were* other reasons for kids to play hockey. Being athletic, being a part of a team, making friends, working on goals, gaining confidence, following through on what you started, having focus, and so much more. He might want to play on his high school hockey team, or later at university, perhaps some day even teach or coach hockey. Of course, my husband knew this was true, but he didn't take much comfort in those possibilities.

One night we caught a game with a few hockey friends, and our kids and everyone was asking what everyone else would be doing next season. Everyone seemed set; they seemed sure of exactly what they'd be doing. Except us. I started wondering what it would be like to declare (admit?) that we might willingly be dropping down a level. Would these hockey fanatics even still relate to us at that point? Would they think we had lost our minds? Hockey families are all about going up, up, up. The only reason you'd drop down a level is if you absolutely couldn't find a spot on a team at the higher level. I often felt it was bragging rights for parents ... what team, level, etc. their child played on. It was so wrong, but it happened. Everyone talked. Everyone checked out where your kid's team stood. I know because we did it too. "I heard Devin made the Stars, you know they're in second place out of ten teams!"

March was almost over, and we still had no idea what Zak really wanted, how much we should push him, or what to do. A few things were definite: we didn't want to have a year of *dragging* him out to his hockey practices and games. If he wanted it, we wanted it, but if he wasn't so motivated maybe it was time to lessen the load. And ... we needed to make up our minds before all the try-outs and potential offers started coming our way. I felt that if we hadn't decided—thoughtfully and firmly—that it would be tempting to automatically go along with something that might've been a dream offer in the past. And if that wasn't what Zak truly wanted this time around, we didn't want that either.

Wouldn't you know that the year we didn't really push for anything was the year offers started pouring in? Weeks before try-outs, A and AA teams came knocking at our door. This, of course, made the decision even harder for my son and seemed to reopen the 'wound' for my husband: how could Zak *think* of saying no to all these magical offers? I felt it too, but not in such an angry way. Hearing that other hockey families we knew were arguing about similar issues made me feel we weren't the only couple in danger of divorcing over our 13-year-old's hockey life! Some offers would have been a dream to us in past years - these were teams we had practically begged to be on! I wanted to tell these coaches YES! I think I did even respond to some of them, "If I were a 13-year-old boy, I would *so* be there, but ... "

Nine

Into Overtime

I 've never felt so Canadian in my life! I pull on my big wooly Roots socks, throw my hockey bag and stick in the trunk, and drive through ice and snow to a late-night hockey game. Drake is blasting in the car ... dammit, I feel like Miss Canada! The same way I feel like part of a super-Canadian *family* when we all roll out of bed at 6 am, pull on toques to hide our bed-hair, and grab some Timmies on our way to an early morning hockey practice. Or how we now rush home from Zak's Saturday hockey games to kick back, crack open a cold one (or some less-adult beverage), and catch a Leafs game on TV together. And I'm not sure I ever would have felt this connected to my 'Canadian-ness' if it hadn't been for my Egyptian husband. What a beautiful thing to be reminded of, to have something of your own 'given back' to you through someone else's point of view.

Learning to skate and play hockey is one of the few places you're encouraged to actually learn how to fall down and then quickly get back up over and over again. Falling down smack hard on your butt is not considered a bad thing on the ice. A hockey instructor once told us that if we weren't falling, we weren't taking enough risks with our hockey drills. So often we're taught that falling down or failing at something in life is bad, and we end up scared to try for fear of failing. One of the very first things you learn in hockey is the valuable lesson of how to fall down and get back up like it's nothing. Even the biggest hockey pros fall on the regular trying to score, skate hard up the ice, or get past a strong opponent. So many hockey lessons cross over into real life for me, and this is one of the most important.

> *"Once you've tried learning hockey as an adult, nothing seems impossible!"*

You try something on the ice over and over again, a move or maneuver that seems impossible—for me it's crossovers or stopping on my left side ... well, there's also stick-handling and shooting, the list could go on! You fall down dozens of times, getting up eager to try again, learning as you go. You're back at the rink the next day, maybe still falling down, getting up again, working and developing confidence in your self and your skills. How can that fail to seep into your real life ... your career, your family, everything? You become less worried about failing; it becomes just a step-up to where you want to be. You understand that you may fail on the first, second, or even hundredth try, but at some point, the magic moment will click and you'll be putting one skate over the other as you tear around that red circle on the ice. Once you've tried learning hockey as an adult, nothing seems impossible!

To me, the hockey world is a microcosm of Canadian culture: diversity and racism forever knocking heads, new views and old bumping up against one another, reaching for something better ... Canadian pride and celebration of other wonderful cultures holding hands, ever-changing and evolving, hopefully for the better.

Hockey isn't perfect.

Canada isn't perfect.

My kids aren't perfect.

I'm not perfect.

Nobody's perfect.

But I like to think we are always striving to grow and be better with each new day, month, and year.

As soon as my youngest son could stand on his own and take a few steps, everyone assumed we'd have him out there skating. When he was still crawling, fellow hockey parents used to ask if we'd bought him skates yet. Jad was practically born into an arena:

as an infant he'd slept through Zak's games in his carrier, he drove us crazy running around on the bleachers when he was a toddler, and all vacations of his young life had been to his older brother's hockey tournaments. So, when he was three, we bought him his own adorably tiny pair of Bauer hockey skates! Now that we were more in the know about hockey, our plan was to start Jad on hockey way earlier than Zak. This time around I knew we weren't *just* learning to skate—I knew this was the start of a whole new hockey player.

But maybe – just maybe – it would go a little differently from now on. My husband and I found ourselves frequently engrossed in conversation about how much we'd learned about dealing with kids in hockey. The good, the bad, and the ugly ... what we feel we did wrong ... when we pushed too much and perhaps made hockey too serious or stressful for Zak ... times we could've kept it more fun. We talked about how much we had learnt about ourselves and our child through these hockey years. About being hockey parents ... and about the hockey parents we wanted to become. My husband shared something a coach (actually the coach who cut us) said to him 'way back when we first started: "You won't get it with your first child, but it's all going to make a whole lot more sense with your second child." A casual remark that seemed insignificant at the time, but that had somehow stayed with him, and now made perfect sense. Words of wisdom. And so we vowed to change gears and move forward with a whole fresh attitude for both our boys' hockey adventures.

I was excited to register us for a weekly parent-tot skating class. Here parents are on the ice with their three-to-five-year-olds, helping them through the class. It sounded like a fun idea! Jad was a shy, clingy toddler, so I couldn't see him being comfortable doing a class on his own anyway. I didn't understand why my more seasoned mom friends weren't as excited about the idea of the parent-tot classes. "Why would you want to do that?" they asked, or "Can't he learn to skate without you? My kids started at three, but I just put them in a class on their own." But I knew my son and couldn't imagine just throwing him onto the ice on blades. Alone. Without me. Plus … wouldn't this be such a fun quality time for us? I envisioned us gliding around the ice hand-in-hand, matching jerseys and all. The reality didn't quite match up with my fantasies. Jad would cry through gearing up and getting ready, then we'd stumble out onto the ice together, where I'd absolutely wreck my back semi-holding him up through the whole class. Instructors encouraged us to let go of our children more, but the kids kept grabbing on for dear life. We'd spend the thirty-minute class 'skating' around pylons and swooping down to pick up colourful balls from one end of the rink and dropping them in a basket far away at the other end of the rink. Kids and parents were falling right and left. There was lots of crying (yeah, probably both kids and parents). At the end of each session, I'd feel a solidarity with all the other parents who had just gone through the same experience and now had to get all the cold, wet snowsuits and skates off their miserable, squirming children. After that course finished, next up was Fun Skates every now and then with Jad. This did turn out to be a little more 'fun', as he gained some small degree of confidence on the ice.

It's the much anticipated first day of real hockey for Jad, now five years old. My phone alarm blasts out at me at 6 am, then again at 6:10, and 6:20; finally, before the 6:30 ring, my husband groans, "You need to get up," rolls over, and resumes snoring. I drag myself out of bed, wake my son up, and we start getting ready for his very first actual hockey practice. This day has been a long time coming. After having watched his older brother play for years, Jad is excited to finally be trying this hockey thing out for himself!

It's a freezing morning, and we shiver in the car waiting for it to warm up enough to start driving. Jad munches on a slice of reheated leftover pizza, I sip black coffee from my thermos, and Drake and The Weekend softly sing to us through the radio as we make our way into the cold, black morning.

"The moon is still out—it's almost FULL!" Jad yelps, peering out and pointing up into the darkness.

I flip-flop about whether all the equipment and gearing up is a curse or a beautiful thing with hockey. Some days I revel in the ritual, other days it irritates me. It's not like any other sport. Think about gearing up for basketball or soccer, where all you really need are running shoes and some sporty clothes, plus a ball and a hoop or net. With hockey it's all skates, chest protector, elbow pads, neck guard, hockey pants, hockey socks, shin guards, jock or jill, helmet, mouthguard, stick, puck, net, tape, ice! One of the newer players on my hockey team actually uses a handy checklist of all the pieces that she uses to pack her bag and get dressed. Last night, getting geared up was a meaningful ritual for me. I was mentally preparing for my game as I taped my hockey socks, chatting with my teammates as I tied my skates, and checking out the gorgeous freshly-Zambonied arena ice as I tightened my helmet strap.

Today we walk into the changeroom full of five-year-olds all dressed and ready to go. Some parents are leisurely putting the final touches on——tightening skates, taping shin pads, fastening helmets. Some kids have already gone out to line up at the rink gate, but no one is totally not dressed like my son. Mornings like this morning make me think, "Why are we involved in a sport with so much gear, so much prep, so much … This is stupid!" Tossing that thought aside, I squeeze Jad in between two kids and frantically start the process. "Mommy, I want to put it on myself!" Jad screams. "This helmet hurts!" By the end of the whole ordeal, I'm drenched in sweat, my back aches, and I expect a standing ovation from the crowd that's been watching our whole show. But as I gather myself back together and stand up, all I see are a few parents quickly averting their glance from this circus that was us. We start walking out of the changeroom, and I notice Jad's stick isn't in the corner with everyone else's. "Did we bring your stick?" I ask Jad. "I don't think so." Oops. Luckily a player practising before us lends us a stick, and all is right in the world once more. Jad lines up to go on the ice, and I head towards the stands to watch.

By the time I find a spot in the stands, most of the other parents are already attentively watching their junior hockey stars, some standing, faces pressed up against the Plexiglass, cameras out, looking totally crazy. But I get it ... the kids are so cute out there. This is my second hockey child, so I'm a little more chill. One kid is making snow angels, another is rolling his uniformed body off the ice towards the door. My guy shuffles along in little running steps between falls. I overhear two toque-wearing hockey moms behind me, "They look sharp in black, don't they?" "They do! Check out that stick-handling!" I wonder for a moment if they're watching the same practice as I am: can they be for real!? I hope they're just being funny. The toque moms go on to discuss the strengths and weaknesses of a few of the five-year-olds and how they heard the coach is going to use "advanced strategies" to make this team the best! Just as I almost turn around to giggle with them, I realize they might actually be serious.

Watching these little kids skate over to a million fun foam shapes the coaches throw all over the ice, work on their stops, get down, pick up a foamy, and skate back to put it in the bin, I can't help wondering why they don't have an adult version of this class. There are lots of beginner adult hockey players like me who would love this and benefit from this type of drill. Probably more than all these advanced (to me) skills and drills and 'learn-to-hockey' classes that people who've been skating and playing for years attend. This is what I need—a total beginner class with foam-toy gathering and being pulled along the ice on my tummy by my teacher's hockey stick as a reward for all my hard skating work.

Leaving the rink, which is near the waterfront of our town, we squint at the sun that is just coming up. A fresh new day on the horizon. We drive into a dazzling sunrise, warm like the rich black coffee in my hand. Here we go—hockey 2.0 (or I guess, 3.0). We both sing along to the radio ... Drake again ... "Started from the bottom, now we're here..."

Acknowledgments

First and foremost, thank you to my sons Zak and Jad, who inspire me and teach me so much about both life and hockey.

Thank you to my husband for showing me Canada through his rose-coloured glasses, introducing me to hockey, and making sure I didn't chicken-out of my very first game!

Thank you to my mom for being mega-supportive and encouraging me to follow whatever crazy dream I might dream up ... including writing this book. And for being an avid hockey mom to a beginner 40-year-old player!

So much love to a few of my very special hockey parent friends who have been there through it all: Erin, Ed, Steve, Norma, Pavel, and Valerie. Our kids have all been on different teams for years now, but the bond remains. Shout-outs to all the other amazing hockey moms and dads I've met through the years on various teams. Of course, thank you to the awesome coaches and trainers we've had the pleasure of working with – you really make a difference!

Hugs and high-fives to all the strong, inspiring hockey women teammates I've had throughout the years. Thank you for making me feel welcome on your teams as a true beginner, pushing me out onto that ice, telling me where to stand at face-offs, and continually cheering me on!

Thanks to all my non-hockey friends who humour me and listen to me talk *way* too much about skates, tournaments, hockey drama, and writing this book!

Made in United States
North Haven, CT
15 August 2022

22740720R00089